# NIKITA
# KHRUSHCHEV

# NIKITA KHRUSHCHEV

BY MICHAEL KORT

Franklin Watts
New York London Toronto Sydney
An Impact Book 1989

To my mother

Photographs courtesy of:
Sovfoto: pp. 13, 24, 62, 91, 123, 147, 150 (A. Slesinger);
Sovfoto/Novosti: pp. 21, 23, 99; Sovofoto/Tass: pp. 32 (both),
45, 71; Eastfoto/Jeno Papp: p. 133.

Library of Congress Cataloging-in-Publication Data

Kort, Michael.
Nikita Khrushchev / Michael Kort.
p.   cm.—(An Impact book)
Bibliography: p.
Includes index.
Summary: Follows the life of the man who was head of the
Soviet Union from 1958 to 1964.
ISBN 0-531-10776-0
1. Khrushchev, Nikita Sergeevich, 1894-1971—Juvenile literature.
2. Heads of state—Soviet Union—Biography—Juvenile literature.
3. Communists—Soviet Union—Biography—Juvenile literature.
[1. Khrushchev, Nikita Sergeevich, 1894-1971.   2. Heads of state.]
I. Title.
DK275.K5K67   1989
947.085'2'092—dc20
[B]
[92]   89-9184   CIP   AC

# CONTENTS

# NIKITA
# KHRUSHCHEV

# ONE

# A YOUTH IN
# OLD RUSSIA

As the nineteenth century was drawing to a close, the Russian Empire stood alone, as it had for centuries, as the giant among the nations of the world. It stretched from Germany and Austria-Hungary in the center of Europe eastward to China and the Pacific coast, where Asia comes to an end 6,000 miles (9,600 km) away. Chilled in the north by the frosty waters of the Arctic Ocean, it was also warmed by the sun-bathed waters of the Caspian Sea 1,500 miles (2,400 km) to the south. Altogether, the Russian Empire occupied about $8\frac{1}{2}$ million square miles (22,100,000 km²), almost three times the area of any other country and more than one seventh of the land area of the entire world.

Within its borders one could find endless tracts of frozen tundra where trees never grew, as well as the largest forests in the world. There were mountains whose peaks soared into the clouds and prairies whose flatness sprawled farther than the eye could see. The empire contained mighty rivers and stagnant marshlands, crystal-clear lakes and salty inland seas, broad expanses of fertile farmland and vast, barren deserts.

The Russian Empire was as varied in population as it was geographically. Only about half of its people were Russian, or Great Russian as they are sometimes called. The rest, conquered or annexed over the centuries, were a diverse collection. Among them were Ukrainians ("Little Russians") and Belorussians ("White Russians"), two groups closely related to the Great Russians. But their languages, while quite similar to Russian, are distinct, as is their historical experience. In addition the Russian Empire included Poles, Latvians, Lithuanians, Estonians, Armenians, Jews, Uzbeks, Turkmenians, Georgians, Kazakhs, and many others, over one hundred distinct ethnic groups in all. The total population of 140 million—while less than China's or India's—was by far the largest of any European state, approximately equal to the populations of Great Britain, France, and Germany combined.

Despite its size, unmatched natural resources, and large population, the Russian Empire was a troubled land. Its government was outdated, inefficient, and often brutal. The emperor—called the tsar—held virtually absolute power. This frustrated and angered many of his subjects, especially the growing number of educated people who compared their country to the more democratic countries of Western Europe. Some of them held liberal beliefs and hoped that their country could gradually reform and improve itself. To make Russia more prosperous, they wanted it to copy the capitalist economic system that existed in the West. To improve Russia's political system, they wanted Russia to establish an elected parliament similar to those in the West. These generally moderate people first began to make their voices heard during the nineteenth century.

The problem was that none of the various tsars was willing to share power with anyone. Anyone who publicly called for reforms risked long jail sentences. Therefore, as early as the 1820s, some of Russia's educated people, convinced that things would never get better under the tsarist system, had turned to the idea of a revolution as the solution to Russia's problems.

During the next seventy years small groups of revolutionaries were able to cause some damage, including assassinating one tsar, Alexander II, in 1881. But the system survived, and the small groups of revolutionaries who dared to challenge it were either chased into exile, hunted down and imprisoned, or, in a few cases, hanged.

The empire's economic problems were also serious. By the nineteenth century Russia was lagging far behind its rivals in Western Europe in terms of industrial development. At the same time, as new industries were built, the economic progress they brought came at a high human price. For some skilled workers the factory meant a chance at a better life and upward social mobility, but most of the people who toiled in Russia's factories and mines worked under horrible conditions. Workers in late-nineteenth-century Russia, *after* the passage of laws to improve their conditions, often put in eighteen-hour days. Children frequently worked twelve or more hours per day. Many were under ten, and some were as young as three. In many factories they were continuously exposed to toxic fumes. Russia's main coal-mining region, known as the Donbass, where one day a boy named Nikita Khrushchev would go to work, had one of the highest accident rates in Europe.

For their efforts Russian workers earned less than half of the wages of American or British workers. Often these terrible conditions led to protests and strikes. But the Russian government was unwilling to interfere on behalf of the workers and often sent in its police or troops to crush strikes with violence and bloodshed.

Severe as these difficulties were, they were dwarfed by an older and greater problem: the condition of the peasantry. Over five sixths of the empire's people were peasant farmers. They lived in a harsh and unforgiving world. Until the 1860s about half had been serfs, subject to the tyranny of their landlords, while the rest were bound to land owned by the state. In either case, when the peasants were finally given their personal freedom, they remained wretchedly poor. Their farming methods were backward. They could barely raise enough food to feed themselves, much less to pay their huge debts and heavy taxes. As recently as 1891–92 Russia was ravaged by terrible famine.

Although by the last decade of the nineteenth century a few peasants had managed a small measure of prosperity, grinding poverty dominated the countryside. Most peasants lived in filthy, thatch-roofed, vermin-infested mud huts. Their diet was monotonous and lacking in essential vitamins, minerals, and protein. Often the peasants lacked enough of even the coarse rye bread that was the basis of their diet. A health researcher once made the ironic observation that bugs stayed away because the peasant huts contained no food. An army of diseases— typhus, diphtheria, malaria, syphilis—constantly invaded their villages. These brutal conditions took their terrible toll, twisting and warping the peasantry into their own ugly image. Anton Chekhov, one of Russia's greatest writers, sadly and sympathetically reported on what he observed:

> Who keeps the pothouse [tavern] and makes drunkards of the people? The peasant. Who embezzles and drinks up the community, school, and church funds? The peasant. Who steals from his neighbor, sets fire to his property, and bears false witness in court for a bottle of vodka? The peasant. Who . . . is the first to raise his voice against the peasants? The peasant. Yes, to live with them was terrible. Yet they were human beings, and there was nothing in their lives for which one could not find justification: oppressive labor that made the whole body ache at night, cruel winters, poor crops, overcrowding, and no help, and no place from which it could be expected. [1]

Periodically the peasants rose in mass rebellion, killing the hated landlords, burning their estates, spreading terror across the countryside, and sending shudders through Russia's two

*Shackled to land they didn't own,*
*Russian peasants under the tsar led lives steeped*
*in poverty, ignorance, and tyranny.*

major cities, Moscow and St. Petersburg. But the ending was always the same: defeat, merciless repression, and continued misery. By the 1890s many peasants were leaving their farms for part of the year to work in Russia's growing industries. But that new source of income was not enough to break the cycle of poverty that seemed without beginning or end, like the great Russian plain on which the peasants lived, endured, and died.

A year that symbolizes both Russia's old problems and changes on its horizon is 1894. In that year Nicholas II, the man destined to be Russia's last tsar, came to the throne. Meanwhile, a younger man, Vladimir Ulyanov, published his first major political work. Once Nicholas was overthrown, Ulyanov, under the name Lenin, would play the leading role in establishing the new system that would govern Russia till this day. Also in 1894, a teenager named Joseph Djugashvili entered a theological seminary, where he soon turned from religion to revolution. Under his adopted name, Stalin, he would succeed Lenin and rule as a tyrannical dictator for a generation.

And on April 17 of that same year, 1894, a peasant boy was born in the village of Kalinovka. For him it would have been a great luxury to be born in a simple log cabin, like some American presidents who were proud of their humble origins. Instead, this child was born in a typical Russian peasant home: a mud hut with a thatch roof. His chances of surviving the hardships of a Russian peasant's childhood and reaching adulthood, much less becoming a major historical figure, were slim. Yet he would live to witness the revolution that toppled the tsar, see Lenin lead his Bolshevik party to power, serve as a key leader under Stalin, and eventually succeed Stalin and begin to heal some of the deep wounds the dictator had left behind. His name was Nikita Sergeyevich Khrushchev.

Kalinovka was located about 225 miles (360 km) south of Moscow. While a majority of the population of that region were Russian, about 20 percent were Ukrainian. The local dialect reflected this ethnic mixture. It was Russian but a Ukrainianaccented Russian that included many Ukrainian words. The ethnic origins of the Khrushchev family are not entirely clear. They considered themselves Russian and spoke the local version of Russian, but the family may have had Ukrainian roots. Like his less famous friends and neighbors, Nikita Khrushchev's accent always marked him as a native of this ethnically mixed region, even though his Russian became much improved in later years. As for Ukrainian, Khrushchev claimed that he learned to speak it "rather well," an opinion that most native Ukrainian speakers probably would not share.

Khrushchev would have good reason to speak Ukrainian as well as possible. The Ukraine, a fertile region of Russia of about 230,000 square miles (598,000 km²) that begins about 50 miles (80 km) from where Khrushchev was born, would play a major part in his life. In later years there he would labor in the coal industry, fight in two wars, and eventually govern for the national government based in Moscow. One difficulty he would face is that many Ukrainians do not like being controlled by Russians. Although the Ukraine was conquered by the Russian state during the seventeenth and eighteenth centuries, resentment toward Russian domination has never been snuffed out there. In fact, Ukrainians proudly point out that the first culture and state considered to be "Russian" had its center in the city of Kiev, in the Ukraine, over a thousand years ago. This ethnic pride was a major problem for the Russian tsar before Nikita Khrushchev was born, and it remains one for the Soviet government almost two decades after his death.

Whatever his precise ethnic origins, it is certain that Nikita Khrushchev came from peasant stock. He provided this bit of family history to a group of foreign visitors:

*I am a Russian of peasant stock. My grandfather was a serf, the property of a landlord who could sell him if he wished, or trade him for a hunting dog. He could neither read nor write, and he had a hard life. He had a bath two times in all his years—once when he was christened as a baby, again when the neighbors prepared him for his burial.* [2]

Nikita's father, Sergei, certainly was a typical peasant. He worked as a farmhand. Like so many other peasants, Sergei's work on the land did not provide enough food to feed his family. Therefore, each winter Sergei left his family and traveled southeast for over 300 miles (480 km) into the Ukraine to a region called the Donbass. There in the town of Yuzovka he worked as a laborer in Russia's most important coal-producing area. Sergei's efforts in the mines did not noticeably improve his fortunes. As his son Nikita recalled, Sergei never reached his goal of being able to buy a horse so that "he could raise enough potatoes and cabbage to feed his family." [3]

Sometimes young Nikita accompanied his father to Yuzovka. At other times he remained behind with his family at his grandfather's home in Kalinovka.

Wherever he lived, young Nikita soon learned to carry his own weight. As he put it, "I started to work as soon as I could walk." [4] He began in Kalinovka guarding the animals of the village, later taking a job herding a prosperous landlord's cows. Nikita also was given at least one early lesson in Russian civics. He was caught fishing by the gamekeeper at the landlord's pond, beaten with a whip, and taken to the police. There he was beaten again, and his fishing pole was taken away.

In Yuzovka, Nikita worked after school and on Saturdays cleaning industrial boilers. This was harrowing work, especially for young boys. As a former coworker recalled many years later:

*It was a miserable man-killing job, for the fires had just been drawn, and the furnace's walls were still so hot your skin blistered, and you could barely breathe when you crawled inside.*

*I recall vividly the day that . . . [one worker] had crawled on his belly through an open hole, and perhaps for three minutes he chipped away at the slag with an iron bar. Then he fell out half alive, gulping air greedily. Then Nikita Sergeyevich entered. For a moment we could see him, thrashing about on the hot bricks like a live fish in the pan. Then he too scrambled out, choking for breath and covered with soot and gray with ash.* 5

Khrushchev reportedly then complained to his boss and was nearly fired for insubordination. Yet harsh working conditions did not keep him from enjoying himself. Nikita seems to have been a strong athlete and outgoing and popular with girls. He was also an excellent dancer, his specialty being the *gopak*, a Ukrainian folk dance.

Until he reached the age of twelve, Nikita's schooling was confined to the winter months. Exactly at what schools he studied is not entirely clear; what is certain is that his education was a limited one. Khrushchev probably first learned to read in a church school in Kalinovka, and then he seems to have attended a village school there run by the state. In his memoirs he also mentions attending school in Yuzovka. At the church school he learned the Gospels extremely well and often quoted from them when he was an important Communist leader. But Khrushchev's intense hostility toward religion, which would be clearly displayed when he became the leader of the Soviet Union, also dates from his childhood Gospel studies. In his memoirs he recalls having to kneel down and pray in front of the icons in church and complains that "when we were taught to read, we read the scriptures."

In contrast, Khrushchev gratefully notes the influence of his teacher in the village school in Kalinovka. She was Lidia Mikhailovna Shchevchenko, who, Khrushchev remembers, "set me on a path which took me away from all that." He adds:

*She was a revolutionary. She was also an atheist. She instilled in me my first political consciousness and began to counteract the effects of my strict religious upbringing.* 6

[ 17 ]

Khrushchev never forgot his debt to his teacher. In 1960, at the height of his power as the Soviet leader and an international figure, he invited her to a New Year's Eve party at the Kremlin, where the tsar had lived when Shchevchenko first took Nikita in hand back in Kalinovka.

In 1908, at the age of fourteen, Khrushchev said good-bye to Kalinovka for good. His father had given up trying to scratch even a part-time living from the soil and decided to work full-time as a miner. He took a job at a mine just south of Yuzovka and moved his entire family there.

Most of the Yuzovka mines were owned by foreigners. While they reaped their profits, the Russians who actually went down into the pits endured work that was hard, dirty, and very dangerous. Wages were low and often not paid on time. The town itself was named after an Englishman, John Hughes, the owner of the company that founded the town in 1869. While the foreign owners and managers lived in the good part of town, called the "English Colony," the Russian miners, whose back-breaking labor brought the coal out of the ground, lived in broken-down huts and barracks, without paved streets, running water, or sewers. Their section of town was called the *Sobachevka—sobaka* means dog in Russian—or "dog settlement." In all of Yuzovka, a community of over forty thousand people, there were three schools, one hospital, one doctor—and thirty-three stores selling alcoholic beverages.

Young Nikita at least escaped the worst working conditions. He had long been interested in mechanical things. Although his father wanted him to be a shoemaker, Nikita tinkered instead with various devices. He once managed to build a motorbike from pieces of scrap. Now Nikita's homespun mechanical skills seem to have paid off. He managed to get a job as an apprentice fitter, or mechanic, at the German-owned Bosse factory. This saved him from having to go down into the coal pits.

In fact, Nikita was on his way up. He was being trained in a skilled trade, one that would allow him to enter the upper crust of the Russian working class. Khrushchev always remained proud of the work he did at the Yuzovka mines and factories and of the skills he mastered. In later years, having risen to the top ranks of the Communist party, he frequently referred to his days as a miner or fitter and was often seen in public wearing a tattered cloth worker's cap. Also, he often began his speeches by announcing, "I am a proletarian (working man)."

Nikita's horizons were widening in other ways as well, especially after he met a miner named Pantelei Makhinya. Unlike most of his coworkers, Pantelei was literate and well read. He was also a poet; many years later, in 1959, Khrushchev would recite one of his poems at a major meeting of Soviet writers in Moscow. Aside from literature, Pantelei introduced Nikita to political writings, including a small volume called *The Communist Manifesto*, the famous and fiery pamphlet by Karl Marx and Friedrich Engels calling for the overthrow of capitalism and its replacement by communism.

Under his friend's influence Khrushchev became an "avid reader," not only of Russian literature and political writing but of foreign literature as well.[7] Among the books he read that most influenced him was Emile Zola's *Germinal*, a vivid description of the harsh lives of miners in France. As Khrushchev later recalled:

> *When I read Emile Zola's* Germinal, *I thought that he was writing not about France, but about the mine in which my father and I worked. The worker's lot was the same both in France and in Russia.*[8]

Meanwhile there were other, greater forces pushing Nikita in a revolutionary direction. In 1904, four years before the Khrushchevs moved permanently to Yuzovka, Russia got into a war with Japan, a war that brought the Russian people nothing but defeat and hardship. The war led to a great upheaval known as the 1905 Revolution. Massive strikes erupted in St. Petersburg, in other major cities, and in Yuzovka and other industrial towns. Military units mutinied. Khrushchev undoubtedly saw and may well have participated in the peasant violence that swept the countryside, including the region around Kalinovka. Nor could he have missed witnessing the brutal repression that finally restored order in late 1905 and 1906.

The 1905 Revolution had some concrete results. Before he was able to restore order, Tsar Nicholas II was forced to grant his subjects a constitution that offered them a little protection and a parliament with limited powers. But in 1911 trouble began to erupt again. The revolutionary groups that the government had crushed but not totally destroyed after 1905 began to recover. Among them were two parties that considered themselves followers of Karl Marx. One was called the Mensheviks and the other, led by Lenin, the Bolsheviks. By 1912 both groups, along with another socialist party called the Socialist Revolutionaries, were organizing in Yuzovka, as well as in other industrial centers across Russia.

That year, sparked by a massacre of workers during a strike in the goldfields of distant Siberia, a new wave of strikes began in Russia. It reached Yuzovka in 1913. Among the thousands of workers swept up in its fury was the fitter Nikita Khrushchev.

Khrushchev seems to have played a fairly minor role in the strike that broke out in the Bosse factory. Probably he was no more than a messenger. But the police net caught even the small fry. Khrushchev was fired from his job and found himself unable to get another at any of the local factories. Still, he was a skilled worker with valuable mechanical skills. That landed him a position at the French-owned Rutchenkovo mines, not as an ordinary miner but as the man responsible for maintaining the elevator that lowered and lifted the miners from the pits.

Nikita settled into his new job. Soon his life took on another dimension of stability. In 1914 he married a young woman named Galina. The new couple managed to find a small

Russia's defeat at the hands of the Japanese
triggered massive civil unrest that culminated in the
1905 Revolution. Workers in major cities took
to the streets, as shown in this demonstration held
in Moscow in October 1905.

but comfortable apartment. But the Khrushchevs were not to enjoy their domestic quiet for long. Dark clouds already loomed overhead, a huge storm about to break. The year was 1914, and World War I was about to explode on Russia and the other nations of Europe.

The full force of the war did not hit Khrushchev. Over one third of the miners were drafted into the army, but since Nikita was a skilled worker, he was spared. However, there was no shortage of trouble for those who remained at home. The defeats and hardships of the war soon led to new strikes in Russia's industrial centers. In the Donbass the strikes began in 1915 and continued on and off until the government was overthrown in 1917. Khrushchev probably was involved in several strikes during 1915 and 1916 but in a minor capacity. By 1915 he was a regular reader of the Bolshevik newspaper, *Pravda*. Still Khrushchev never did enough to get arrested, and books written later by Soviet historians, which certainly would have cited any significant Khrushchev involvement, do not mention him by name.

Khrushchev may have been more involved in domestic affairs. He and Galina soon had two children. A son, Leonid, was born in 1916; tragically, he would be killed in action while serving as a pilot at the pivotal battle of Stalingrad in World War II. A daughter, Yulia, followed in 1918; she survived until 1981.

As it turned out, along with millions of ordinary Russians who were slaughtered, the tsarist government would not survive World War I. By early 1917, bled by 6 million soldiers killed and wounded, tormented by hunger that grew worse each day, and infuriated by a government that ignored all calls for reform, the Russian people could take no more. In March food riots and strikes in the capital, Petrograd—as St. Petersburg had been renamed in 1914 (today called Leningrad)—spread out of control. Troops called to restore order joined the strikers and rioters instead. Within a week the government collapsed. Tsar

The 1917 Revolution resulted in the abdication
of Tsar Nicholas II. Shown here are soldiers
(foreground) and peasants alike demonstrating
in Leningrad (formerly Petrograd).

A crowd of demonstrators in Leningrad disperses
after being attacked by police and soldiers of
Aleksandr Kerensky's revolutionary government. Four
months later, in November 1917, Kerensky's regime
would be overthrown by the Bolshevik Revolution.

Nicholas was forced to abdicate, and a democratic government was proclaimed.

The new government was made up of moderate and liberal men who believed in Western-style democracy. It called itself the Provisional Government, as it expected to govern only until nationwide elections could provide for a new constitution and government based on popular consent.

A telegram brought the news of the revolution to the Rutchenkovo mines. The collapse of the old government left a power vacuum, so workers began to organize their own councils—known as "soviets" in Russian—to manage their affairs. They also organized their own armed militias to protect themselves. Khrushchev emerged as one of the leaders of the Rutchenkovo soviet and may have been its chairman. One of his first tasks was to take charge of arresting the local tsarist police and helping to form an armed workers' militia.

None of these actions settled very much. The old system of government, one that had lasted for hundreds of years, was gone. Although a group of businessmen and intellectuals in the capital claimed to be the new government, in fact nobody controlled most of Russia. The country was involved in the bloodletting of World War I. All sorts of factions were struggling for position in the chaos, which grew worse as 1917 wore on.

A new world of choices and possibilities—and dangers—had opened up for millions of former subjects of the fallen tsar. Most of them, while hopeful, were confused and frightened. Nikita Khrushchev was one of the millions in the vast majority who had yet to cast their lot with one faction or another during 1917. Even in November, when news came from Petrograd that Lenin and the Bolsheviks had overthrown the Provisional Government and seized power themselves, Khrushchev did not commit himself. He was soon to do so, however, in a decision that put him on a long and dangerous road, one that eventually took him from Kalinovka to the Kremlin.

# TWO
# A MAN IN
# NEW RUSSIA

It is difficult to imagine a country in greater turmoil than Russia late in 1917. It was locked in the death grip of World War I, which continued to squeeze the life out of the country. The Provisional Government had tried its best to cope with the crisis. But the burden of fighting the war, establishing democratic institutions, restoring public order, and feeding and sheltering a cold and hungry people was too heavy, and the government was easily overthrown by the Bolshevik party after only eight months. The Bolshevik government set up in November promised that it would provide "Land, Bread, and Peace," but its effective authority during its first days was limited to little more than Petrograd and Moscow. Elsewhere, anarchy ruled.

Although the new Bolshevik government faced the same problems of war, disorder, and suffering as the defunct Provisional Government had, its goals were radically different. The leaders of the Provisional Government wanted Russia to follow the example of Western Europe and the United States. They believed in political democracy, in an economic system based on capitalism and the free market, and in sticking with the democratic nations—led by Great Britain, France, and the United States—in their war against Germany and its partners.

The Bolsheviks, led by Vladimir Lenin, a man with an extraordinary combination of political skill, intelligence, flexibility, and plain ruthlessness, hated the Western democracies and everything they stood for. As Marxists, the Bolsheviks wanted to destroy capitalism and replace it with socialism. Under socialism an orderly plan, rather than the brutal marketplace, would control the economy. The wealth of society would be held in common, rather than in private hands. Inequality, under which extreme wealth existed alongside terrible poverty, would be replaced by equality and fairness.

A key question was how to achieve all of this, and here the Bolsheviks differed not only from the supporters of capitalism but from many socialists as well. Lenin was convinced that only his party, under his leadership, could build socialism in Russia. He was determined that the Bolsheviks alone should rule Russia, without interference from any other organized political groups, whether they called themselves socialist, communist, or anything else. What was crucial to Lenin and the Bolsheviks, as it had been to many other Russian revolutionaries, going back several generations, was not that the government was democratically chosen but that it represented the working people of Russia. Nor did Lenin listen to the objection that it was impossible to know, without an election, who actually represented Russia's working masses. He insisted that only the Bolsheviks could do the job, regardless of any election results. For centuries Russia had suffered under a tsarist dictatorship that had hurt the people; now it would prosper under a Bolshevik dictatorship that would help the people.

This insistence on establishing a one-party dictatorship quickly led to trouble. Shortly after the Bolsheviks seized power, a national election for a constitutional assembly was held. It had been scheduled by the Provisional Government, and not even the Bolsheviks dared cancel it. They received about a quarter of the vote, finishing in second place behind the Socialist Revolutionaries, who received just under half of the vote. The Bolshevik response to their defeat in the only free election in Russia's history was swift. When the selected assembly met in January 1918, Bolshevik gunmen closed it down by force.

Meanwhile, those the Bolsheviks proposed to exclude from power—from supporters of the deposed monarchy to socialists who agreed with many of the Bolshevik economic goals—began to organize. They opposed the Bolsheviks for a variety of reasons beyond the question of the Bolshevik dictatorship. Many nationalistic Russians, for example, bitterly opposed the Bolshevik decision to end the war with Germany at any price, a step that led to a peace treaty in March 1918. Often those opposed to the Bolsheviks could agree on little else and actually fought among themselves. At one point the anti-Bolsheviks totaled no less than eighteen "governments" and factions. Making matters more complex, the Western powers supported the anti-Bolsheviks with arms, money, and even small numbers of troops.

By the middle of 1918, just released from the carnage of world war, Russia was plunged into something even worse—civil war. For the next three years the country was torn apart. Russian armies fought other Russian armies without mercy. Peasants killed landlords and often fought each other over the spoils. Guerrilla forces and bandit gangs preyed on whatever victims they could find. People fought each other for scraps of food, tore down houses and ripped apart wooden sidewalks in the desperate search for fuel, and huddled together to warm themselves with their bodies when nothing else was available. It was a time, as historian William Henry Chamberlin wrote, "when hunger, cold, disease, and terror stalked through the country like the Four Horsemen of the Apocalypse. . . . one of the greatest explosions of hatred, or rather hatreds . . . ever witnessed in human history."[1]

In this war of all against all, old values seemed useless and irrelevant. Simple people struggled to find their way, choosing the side with which they could agree or that could at least offer them protection, and survive. In Yuzovka, as in the rest of the Ukraine, the choice was not easy. Although after November 1917 the Bolsheviks were in control in Petrograd and Moscow and claimed to be the legitimate government for all of Russia, in Yuzovka the Mensheviks and Socialist Revolutionaries continued to be the most popular parties.

On top of that, many Ukrainians, like minority ethnic groups throughout Russia, hoped to use the current turmoil to break away from Russia and become independent. In December in Kiev, the Ukraine's largest city and its ancient capital, a group of Ukrainian leaders declared the Ukraine independent. This did not prevent Bolshevik forces from overrunning the Ukraine in January 1918. After the Russo-German peace treaty that March, the German army, with the support of Ukrainian nationalists, drove the Bolsheviks out and occupied the region themselves.

By late 1917 Khrushchev was leaning toward the Bolsheviks. He certainly must have identified with his fellow miners, who were angered when the Provisional Government supported the mine owners in local labor disputes prior to its overthrow. The miners also knew that since the Bolshevik coup certain anti-Bolshevik forces (called the "Whites," as opposed to the Bolshevik "Reds") led by ex-tsarist generals were being quite rough on miners in areas they controlled. Another factor that probably influenced Khrushchev was the Bolsheviks' decisiveness and willingness to take action at a time when many other political parties seemed paralyzed.

Therefore, before 1917 ended, Nikita Khrushchev enlisted as a member of the local Bolshevik militia, known as the Red Guards. He saw action immediately in the campaign that temporarily established Bolshevik control of the Ukraine in January 1918. But then the Germans came. The Bolshevik forces,

Khrushchev among them, had to run for their lives. Khrushchev's escape had a touch of the dramatic appropriate for a miner. As the Germans closed in, he escaped through a mine shaft, exiting from there into the open prairie, and made his way back to Kalinovka.

Khrushchev's return to his home village duplicated the journeys of many peasants recently turned industrial workers. Their going home reflected the most basic peasant yearning: land. All over Russia, peasants were seizing the estates of the landlords and dividing them up. Everywhere—in the industrial centers, in towns and cities, at the front with the army—beginning in the middle of 1917 peasants abandoned what they were doing and rushed home so as not to miss out on the spoils. When he arrived home in Kalinovka, Khrushchev became one of the leaders of the local peasant soviet that was dividing up the land.

Khrushchev then made official what he had decided on in practice. In April 1918 he formally applied for and was admitted to the Bolshevik party.

Almost immediately, by the summer of 1918, he was back in the heat of battle as a member of the newly formed Red Army. Actually, Khrushchev was not a regular soldier. He was what the Bolsheviks called a political commissar. Although they were not responsible for military decisions, Bolshevik political commissars played a critical role in the fighting. In a struggle in which armies were hastily organized and often disintegrated in the face of danger, much less defeat, Khrushchev and his fellow political commissars had the job of keeping up morale, maintaining discipline, and, most of all, preventing desertion.

The job was extremely difficult. Discipline often collapsed, and desertion was rampant despite the best efforts of the political commissars. Yet Khrushchev performed well, both as a political commissar and as a fighter in the Seventy-fourth Regiment of the Red Army's Ninth Rifle Division. His unit fought against the army led by General Anton Denikin, probably the strongest White military force. Khrushchev endured, as he put it, "severe hardships," especially during a series of defeats and retreats early in 1919. This was followed by decisive victories, as Khrushchev's division, attached to the First Cavalry Army, marched southward "right through a hail of enemy bullets" until they defeated all opposing forces near the shores of the Black Sea. [2]

Among these victories was a famous campaign in the winter of 1919. It marked the debut of the newly formed Bolshevik cavalry. The Bolsheviks also demonstrated their ability to use infantry and cavalry together effectively. While the cavalry struck its lightning blows, the Bolshevik infantry, including Commissar Khrushchev, followed with unexpected speed, pulled over the frozen countryside by horse-drawn sleds.

Khrushchev was also present at a battle whose long-term political consequences were far greater than its military implications. This was the battle in the summer of 1918 over the city of Tsaritsyn, a battle the Bolsheviks won. But the real fight was between two Bolshevik leaders, Leon Trotsky and Joseph Stalin, who within a few years would become the main contenders to succeed Lenin. Although Trotsky and Stalin technically argued over military strategy, the real conflict involved their struggle for political influence and their personal antagonism. Trotsky, the founder and head of the Red Army and the Bolshevik who was second in prestige and power only to Lenin, won that battle. But it proved to be only the first in a long and deadly political war between the two men. It was a war in which Khrushchev was to participate. Its outcome would do a great deal to determine not only his fate but that of millions of Soviet citizens and the revolution itself.

Khrushchev was, and had every reason to be, proud of his role in the Red Army during what he accurately called "the first, most dangerous years of our young Soviet republic." [3] The Red Army's political commissars had to demonstrate courage

under fire and political reliability, and this he did. Yet while he made the grade in a very tough school, Khrushchev did not distinguish himself. His low rank at the end of the Civil War—he was still responsible for only a small unit—contrasts with that of one of his future rivals, Georgi Malenkov. Malenkov, although younger than Khrushchev, rose quickly to become one of the Red Army's top political commissars.

By the end of 1920 the Bolsheviks had won the Civil War. Their problems, however, had only begun. Seven years of world war and civil war had devastated the economy. Factories were ruined and rusting. Mines were abandoned. Worst of all, many farms lay untilled; and where peasants still worked the soil, they often raised food only for themselves. During the fighting the Bolsheviks had been brutal in seizing food and supplies for the Red Army, resorting to forced labor to keep up production wherever they could and violently suppressing any political dissent. Their secret police, the *Cheka*, had terrorized the country. As a result, once the Whites were defeated, the victorious Bolsheviks faced widespread riots, rebellions, and strikes from peasants in the remote countryside to workers in the capital city of Petrograd.

It was into this constant crisis that low-level but reliable party workers like Nikita Khrushchev were thrown in late 1920 and early 1921. Khrushchev was sent back to the Donbass and Yuzovka. The task there was straightforward: get coal production restored so that the country could be warmed and powered. It was a challenge no less difficult than the military challenges of the recent war. Coal production in the Donbass was at one third of prewar levels; one third of all industrial enterprises were destroyed. Although the White armies had gone, Ukrainian

*Leon Trotsky (top) and Joseph Stalin were two ambitious Marxist leaders who later vied for Vladimir Lenin's post as leader of the Bolsheviks.*

nationalist guerrilla bands continued to resist Bolshevik control of their land, which to them was nothing more than the old wine of Russian domination in a new—Bolshevik rather than tsarist—bottle. To top it all, during 1921–22 a terrible famine stalked the land, bringing with it starvation and disease that took millions of lives, among them Khrushchev's young wife, who died in 1921. Conditions were so bad that cannibalism occurred in certain regions, including the Donbass.

The Bolshevik government responded decisively and without pity. It sent one of its toughest leaders, Joseph Stalin, to take charge of the so-called Ukrainian Labor Army, which was nothing more than a forced-labor unit that drafted whomever it needed, from ordinary miners to technical specialists, into its ranks. Khrushchev's position in a sense symbolized the revolution itself. He was made assistant manager at one of the Rutchenkovo mines near Yuzovka, where he had been an employee before the war. His boss, Yegor Abakumov, would later work with him in one of Khrushchev's great triumphs—the building of the Moscow subway—prior to becoming the deputy head of the coal industry of the entire Soviet Union. Aside from the monumental task of restoring the mines, assistant manager Khrushchev had to cope with desertion by workers; lack of food, power, and basic mining machines; and constant attacks by guerrillas and bandits. During one of those attacks he suffered yet another personal loss when his old friend Pantelei Makhinya was killed.

Early in 1921 another major problem arose, this one political and psychological rather than physical or technical. During the Civil War the Bolsheviks had taken control of the entire Russian economy, a policy that came to be known as War Communism. This policy was based on force. To the extent that it kept the Red Army supplied, War Communism can be considered a success. But at the same time it led to economic disaster, as unpaid workers deserted their posts, peasants whose grain was seized refused to plant new crops, and people everywhere began to protest, often violently, against the harshness of the policy. Still, most party workers favored War Communism because it seemed to them that in taking over the economy the Bolshevik state had taken an important step toward socialism.

In the face of growing popular anger and violence directed against his government, and desperate to get industrial and especially food production restored, Lenin changed direction in March 1921. His "New Economic Policy" (NEP) took the government out of most economic affairs. It allowed self-interest and the marketplace to stimulate people, especially the all-important peasants, to work. The government retained control of only the largest industrial enterprises. Most small businesses and Russia's 20 million peasant farms operated in a free market.

For Khrushchev, as for many other party workers, the NEP was demoralizing and hard to accept. It was a step backward from the goal of socialism. Almost immediately, private enterprise and small capitalists began to prosper and, what was far worse, to outperform the state. While Khrushchev reluctantly accepted the NEP as "absolutely necessary" to restore the economy, he and his party comrades found it "difficult and painful for us to adapt ourselves" to the new system:

> We were supposed to defeat the private merchants . . . by beating them at their own game. We tried to take over as much commerce as possible and put it in state hands. We tried hard to underprice the NEP men in state cooperatives and also to offer higher quality and better service. But we didn't have much success. Merchants who were in business for themselves could put up better displays of their products and give their customers better attention. Private stores catered to housewives, who like to have a choice when they shop; they like to browse around and examine everything carefully. [4]

Khrushchev was not alone in his assessment of the NEP. The first to benefit were the peasants, who could grow food and sell it on the free market at high prices. Workers in major industrial enterprises did less well. The mines and large factories took time to repair. Meanwhile, wages were kept low, that is, when they were finally paid. Living conditions were terrible, considerably worse than before the revolution. In Khrushchev's Yuzovka, a local official reported, workers lived "in houses that have no roofs at all . . . workers and their families live beneath open-hearth furnaces and coke ovens."[5] This general picture is confirmed by Khrushchev's own testimony, in which he recalled that as an assistant manager he lived worse than he had as an ordinary worker before the war. When the inevitable strikes broke out, the Bolsheviks suppressed them as mercilessly and violently as had the tsars in years past.

As an assistant mine manager, Khrushchev obviously had to earn his spurs by bringing the workers into line. No doubt he must have tried, as he recalled years later, to "talk" to the striking miners. Nor can one doubt that he believed he was acting for the common good. One witness recalled Khrushchev's taking precisely that line in "talking" to his miners:

> Everything depends on coal. How can the factories produce boots and shirts if they do not have coal? All you demand you must get with your own hands. No manna from the sky is going to come down to you. So beat your picks with all your might.[6]

What is also beyond doubt is that when workers refused to listen to Khrushchev's inspirational speeches, he resorted to force. Otherwise, he would certainly have lost his position.

The NEP did its job. By 1923, after only two years, the situation had improved, not only in the Donbass but in much of the Soviet Union. By 1925 good harvests had eliminated food shortages, and the arrival of modern machinery enabled the Donbass coal mines to raise production dramatically.

Khrushchev meanwhile had made a personal decision that

did as much to improve his career as Lenin's had done to improve the economy. He decided to continue his education. Although he had read widely over the years on his own, his formal education was still limited to his school years in Kalinovka and Yuzovka. This put him at a disadvantage in the competition to earn party promotions above a certain level. Khrushchev, who in later years would demonstrate many times over his ability to size up a political situation, clearly recognized this. There also may have been another element involved: the thirst for and appreciation of education on the part of a man denied one, qualities all too frequently missing in those of us who take educational opportunities for granted. So in 1922 Nikita Khrushchev asked for the chance to go back to school.

This matter was not as simple as it sounds. In the United States an adult's decision to go to work or to school is an individual one. No governmental permission is required. In the Soviet Union it was different. As a party member Khrushchev needed his superior's permission to give up his party-assigned work, even for something as legitimate as furthering his education. Khrushchev was valued for his expertise at the mines and for his dedication to local party work. In 1922 he was offered a promotion to manager at the Pastukhov mines near Yuzovka. Instead, Khrushchev requested to be relieved of his party duties so that he could study at an institution called the Yuzovka Workers' Faculty.

The Workers' Faculty was not an ordinary school. It was part of a large network of schools set up to train party functionaries. These workers were to replace the large numbers of educated people who had left Russia in the wake of the Bolshevik triumph. For Khrushchev, already approaching thirty, the Workers' Faculty represented his last chance to get an education that might open up new career vistas. So when his local party boss refused his initial request, Khrushchev persisted, and after repeated attempts he got his way. In 1922 Nikita Khrushchev—mechanic, political commissar, assistant mine manager—became a student. After four years as a Bolshevik, he finally took his first significant step up the long, slippery, and hazardous party ladder.

Khrushchev attended the Workers' Faculty for three years. He seems not to have been an ordinary student. From the start Khrushchev was a party watchdog inside the student body, assuring that his fellow students followed the directives coming form the party leadership in Moscow. By 1923 this job was formalized with the title of political guide at the school. He obviously did his job well. When he graduated in April 1925, he was appointed party secretary for one of the districts in Stalino, as Yuzovka had recently been renamed.

Meanwhile, Khrushchev had taken another major step. In 1924 he remarried. His new wife was Nina Petrovna Kukharchuk. She was a schoolteacher, with whom he would have three more children and, from all accounts, a warm and happy marriage that lasted almost half a century, until the end of his life.

The political arena that Khrushchev entered in 1925 was a fury-filled ring. Lenin was dead and the struggle to succeed him was raging. In the first round of that struggle most of the party leaders, including Stalin, united against and defeated Trotsky. Thereafter, Stalin manipulated his remaining rivals against each other, eventually emerging victorious over all of them by 1929.

One of Stalin's strengths was his ability to appeal to lower-level party workers. These people often had a limited education, had not been with the party in its early, prerevolutionary days, and were concerned with building careers. They therefore were inclined to support whoever was in a position to help them. Khrushchev was one of those people, a Stalin supporter from the start.

As a district party leader in a regime that was growing increasingly dictatorial, Khrushchev in effect was the mini-dictator of a 400-square-mile (1,040-km²) territory that included one city and several towns and villages. Yet even then he was different from most of his fellow mini-dictators. They generally ruled their regions by sending out commands from their offices. Not Comrade Khrushchev. He insisted on meeting his district's forty thousand people where they lived and worked and on seeing things firsthand. This trait became his political trademark. As he later recalled:

> When I worked as Secretary of a District Party Committee in the Donets basin, I used to go to the villages, and I would get into a sleigh—at that time instead of automobiles there were sleighs—and I would put on a kozhukh [a sheepskin coat], and the frost would not bite me. 7

Another of Khrushchev's trademarks was his enthusiastic and effective support of Stalin. During 1925 he was selected as a delegate to the Ninth Ukrainian Communist Party Congress. A word of explanation is necessary here. Although the Union of Soviet Socialist Republics (USSR) is and always has been a tightly centralized state controlled from Moscow, it claims to be a "union" of republics that have joined up voluntarily. Each republic officially has its own government. Each also officially has its own branch of the Communist Party. Thus, in 1925, within the USSR there was a Ukrainian SSR, and within the Communist Party of the Soviet Union (or "All-Union" Communist Party) there was a Ukrainian Communist Party. In reality, neither body had any independence at all. But the official government of the Ukraine and the local party did in fact govern the Ukraine, although always on orders from Moscow. Real power lay in the hands of the Communist Party of the Soviet Union (CPSU), as the Bolsheviks renamed their party after the revolution.

The head of the Ukrainian Communist Party was Lazar Kaganovich, Stalin's toughest and best troubleshooter. Kaganovich obviously liked what he saw in Khrushchev, for when the Communist Party of the Soviet Union gathered in Moscow at its Fourteenth All-Union Party Congress in December 1925, Khrushchev was there as a nonvoting delegate.

This was Khrushchev's first glimpse of Moscow, an unforgettable event for the peasant/worker from Kalinovka. He was "overjoyed" just to be in fabulous, legendary Moscow. It bothered him not at all that the delegates were housed in crowded barracks, where they slept "on plank beds . . . all stacked together like logs." Nor was he discouraged by his first urban adventure. He immediately became lost on his first streetcar ride to the Kremlin, where the congress met. Thereafter, his behavior was vintage Khrushchev:

> From then on I woke up early and walked to the Kremlin. It took longer, but at least I learned my way around. I even skipped breakfast in order to be sure of arriving on time to get a good seat.[8]

From that seat Khrushchev was able to get close to and admire Stalin, as well as to join in the merciless shouting down of anyone who dared speak against his revered leader. Khrushchev was one of the young toughs who were the battering rams Stalin used to smash his opponents in the struggle for power. Years later he would regard Stalin with hatred and contempt and would take the lead in destroying the dead dictator's reputation. But now he was in awe of the party's new leader. Aside from being a master in behind-the-scenes manipulation, Stalin knew how to play to his audience in public. For example, at a photography session to which a number of ordinary delegates—including Khrushchev—was invited, Stalin criticized the photographer for ordering people around. "No one may order anyone else around ever again," Stalin joked, scoring points with inexperienced loyalists like Khrushchev, who saw Stalin as a genuine man of the people.

After the congress closed, Khrushchev continued his service to Stalin. Stalin was picking off his opponents one by one, rubbing out the remaining traces of free debate in the process. At his first recorded public speech, on November 17, 1926, at a conference of the Ukrainian Communist Party, Khrushchev revealed two qualities vital to survival in the dangerous decade that was to follow. First, the young Stalinist was without pity. When he called for harsher repression against Stalin's opponents, "regardless of their former merits or positions," Khrushchev actually was calling for harsher measures than Stalin had!9 And this was precisely the second invaluable quality he displayed: an ability to sense future political trends. As it turned out, Stalin was soon to take much harsher measures—arrests, expulsions from the party, prison terms, and death sentences— and Khrushchev seems to have anticipated this. Given the treacherous twists and turns that lay hidden on the Stalinist political road ahead, where one miscalculation could and often did prove fatal, Khrushchev's clairvoyance was something every Soviet politician needed.

The next few years gave Khrushchev a chance to use and sharpen his political skills. By 1927 he had moved up from his district job to a post with the Stalino regional organization. Both Khrushchev and the organization had major successes. They increased party membership, raised coal production above prewar levels, and even managed to improve services. The party expanded railway service, built cultural institutions, and put into service the region's first radio transmitter.

There was also trouble, what the party chiefs in Moscow called "moral corruption." Among the charges leveled against the Stalino organization were chronic drunkenness (an age-old Russian problem), and womanizing, including taking advantage of female party workers. Khrushchev's role in this is unclear, but these types of excesses (although he certainly enjoyed drinking and sometimes drank too much) are not what one would expect from him.

He was not seriously hurt by the scandal. In December

1927 Khrushchev was a delegate at the Fifteenth All-Union Party Congress, this time as a voting delegate. He once again took every opportunity to show his devotion to Stalin, as the party chief continued to defeat his opponents. Some of those in the opposition camp were old friends, but Khrushchev never let that bother him. As he put it: "We justified what was happening in lumberjack terms: when you chop down a forest, the chips fly."[10]

In 1928 Khrushchev managed a graceful exit from Stalino when he accepted a post in the city of Kharkov, which at the time was the capital of the Ukraine. Khrushchev was chosen for the job by Stanislav Kosior, then the head of the Ukrainian Communist Party. Kosior wanted Khrushchev because the party wanted to promote people of authentic working-class origins to important positions. The Communist Party, after all, claimed to represent the working class. Yet in those years many key positions still were held by intellectuals of middle-class origin, many of whom tended to be too independent for Stalin's liking. Nikita Khrushchev, at once peasant and industrial mechanic, filled the bill perfectly.

Khrushchev was not happy in his new job. Apparently he had personal conflicts with some veteran party associates in Kharkov. After a few months he readily accepted a transfer to a post in Kiev, the largest city in the Ukraine.

Kiev was actually much more than the Ukraine's largest city. This beautiful city on the Dnieper River was the region's traditional capital and, even more, the center of the first Russian civilization and state from the ninth to the thirteenth century. This was not lost on Khrushchev. His awe for Kiev, the "mother of Russian cities," matched his feelings for Moscow. "As soon as I arrived," he recalled many years later, "I went straight to the banks of the Dnieper and gazed at the famous river with my suitcase still in hand."[11]

Khrushchev's adoring gaze was not returned by the local party apparatus. Despite Stalin's tightening grip on the party, there were still people with the courage and power to make their will known. Some of them were ethnic Ukrainians in the Ukraine party organization. Although they were loyal Communists, their ethnic pride led them to protect the Ukrainian language and culture from being submerged by the Russian tide flowing from Moscow, a battle Ukrainians and other ethnic groups had been fighting before the Revolution and continue to fight today.

It seems that Khrushchev was quickly drawn into that ancient battle that has outlived generations of tsars and dictators. Although Khrushchev remembered that he had "many pleasant memories of that period" and that the people there "seemed to like me and . . . even . . . respected me," he also recalls that some of them considered him a "hopeless 'Rusak,' " Ukrainian slang for Russian.[12]

Soon Khrushchev was agitating to get out of Kiev. To get ahead in the party he needed more training, and an excellent place to get it was at the Stalin Industrial Academy in Moscow. Again he ran into resistance; he was a reliable worker whom no party chieftain wanted to lose. Khrushchev had to go to Ukrainian party boss Kosior. After a number of meetings with Kosior and his aides, Khrushchev received permission to transfer to Moscow. The crucial help Khrushchev needed actually came from Moscow, where former Ukrainian boss Lazar Kaganovich now sat at Stalin's right hand. Kaganovich wanted tough men of authentic working-class origin to staff the party machine. Khrushchev, in terms of both temperament and background, again filled the bill perfectly.

The year was 1929. Stalin had destroyed his last opponents. He had already begun the radical industrialization policies that over the next decade would transform and brutalize the Soviet Union. And Nikita Khrushchev, at thirty-five, stood poised to participate in a process that would propel him to the top of the party hierarchy, even as it claimed the lives of many of his colleagues and millions of innocent people.

# THREE
## THE STALIN
## REVOLUTION

Khrushchev's arrival in Moscow in 1929 coincided with the beginning of one of the most tumultuous decades in Russia's history, the years of what is called the Stalin Revolution. The Stalin Revolution did not involve the overthrow of a system of government, such as had occurred in Russia in 1917. Yet what happened in the Soviet Union between 1929 and 1939 in many ways was more fundamental and far-reaching. The Stalin Revolution was an economic revolution. It was a breakneck industrialization drive, the goal of which was to close the gap, once and for all, between Russia and the more economically advanced countries of the West.

During this drive the Soviet leadership dictated that new industries be built as fast as possible. No cost, no obstacle, no amount of human suffering was allowed to get in the way. The result was that the industrial growth of many decades was squeezed into one. This was a remarkable accomplishment, one that the Soviet Union takes pride in to this day. At the same time, the Soviet people were forced to endure terrible hardship and suffering. These were made all the worse because the

*The Stalin Revolution's goal was to industrialize
Russia almost overnight. Two hundred motorcars, resembling
American-made 1929 Ford automobiles, were manufactured
daily by the Molotov Auto Plant in Gorki. Hanging
from the ceiling is a huge poster of Stalin.*

country was subject to a political tyranny of incredible cruelty and violence, which added enormous pain to millions of lives already tormented beyond endurance.

A comparison of Soviet life in 1929 and 1939 shows how dramatic the Stalin Revolution really was. In 1929, despite the changes of the past twelve years, a great deal still remained as it had been in 1917. Although the landlords were gone and their estates divided up, most people in Russia were still peasant farmers, and their millions of small farms remained the single largest sector of the national economy. The country's major industrial enterprises, although now owned and run by the state, were far fewer than a huge country such as the Soviet Union needed. They could not meet the nation's needs, and they lagged far behind the more modern industries in the West. In short, in 1929 most of the population lived as it had before 1917, while the country as a whole continued to compare unfavorably to the modern industrialized nations of the West.

Ten years later the picture was very different. The individual peasant farms had been replaced by larger units, called collective farms, each of which was worked by hundreds of families. The Soviet Union had built thousands of new industries that enabled it to compete, at least in terms of military power, with the modern industrial countries of Western Europe. A country that had always been rural, an expanse of small villages dotted with a few cities and large towns, was becoming an urban society as peasants poured into rapidly growing cities. An unprecedented outburst of political terror—during which millions of people disappeared forever—had disrupted lives at every level of society and wiped out and replaced most of the country's political leadership. By 1939—after a decade of extraordinary growth and remarkable accomplishments, of disastrous errors and terrible suffering—very few people in the Soviet Union lived as they had only ten years before.

The policies that produced these radical and painful changes began as Stalin was defeating his rivals in the late

1920s. With the party dominated by his supporters, Stalin ended the NEP. It was replaced by a furious, full-speed drive to turn the Soviet Union into a modern industrial nation. The goal was to catch up with the West in ten years. Stalin's excuse for such a frantic pace was that it was necessary to establish socialism firmly in the Soviet Union and to enable it to resist any future attacks by the capitalist nations.

The key to accomplishing this seemingly impossible task was careful planning of the industrialization drive. Economic development would proceed according to a series of five-year plans, which would coordinate the nation's resources in order to make the most of them. The first five-year plan, over one thousand pages long, was issued in 1929. It called for phenomenal increases in production of most goods. Industrial production, for instance, was to go up by 250 percent. Heavy industry, such as coal, steel, and machine tool production, was to jump by 330 percent.

The plan also called for what was called collectivization of agriculture, the combining of small peasant farms into much larger cooperative farms. The expectation was that peasants on these farms would combine their tools and labor and jointly cultivate the land. Because their fields would be much larger, they would be able to make efficient use of machines and modern farming technology. This would increase production and provide the food to feed the new workers in the cities. Surplus crops would be exported to pay for modern industrial machinery.

Collectivization was vital to the five-year plans because it was supposed to increase production and give the government more control over what was produced. After all, it would be much easier to control 200,000 large collective farms than 20 million scattered peasant farms. There was one major problem, however. The peasants wanted to keep their own farms, no matter how small. The result was a terrible slaughter. The peasants were torn from their farms by force. Those who tried to resist were killed. Often entire villages were machine-gunned to break peasant resistance. The following eyewitness account of a peasant revolt is typical of what happened:

> For three days . . . a bloody battle was waged between the revolting people and the authorities. . . . This revolt was cruelly punished. Thousands of peasants, workers, soldiers, officers paid for the attempt with their lives, while the survivors were deported to concentration camps. . . . mass executions were carried out near the balkis [ravines]. The soil of this region was soaked in blood. After the executions, these villages were set on fire. [1]

Some peasants escaped being placed on the collective farms, but their fate was even worse. These were the more prosperous peasants, or *kulaks*. The *kulaks*, along with their wives and children, were killed or deported to remote areas of the Soviet Union or to the country's rapidly expanding network of slave-labor camps. Often entire families committed suicide. They thereby avoided a fate that was often little better:

> Trainloads of deported peasants left for the icy North, the forests, the steppes, the deserts. These were whole populations, denuded of everything; the old folk starved to death in mid-journey, newborn babies were buried on the banks of the roadside, and each wilderness had its crop of little crosses of boughs of white wood. [2]

Having taken millions of lives already, collectivization was crowned, in a sense, by famine. In 1932 the turmoil and desperate peasant resistance produced a poor harvest. The problem was centered in the Ukraine, Khrushchev's old territory. Despite the poor harvest, the government continued to take what grain there was in the Ukraine, leaving the local peasants nothing for themselves. They ate cats, dogs, field mice, bark, and even horse manure ("We fight over it. Sometimes there are whole grains in it," a peasant woman told a party worker) in a losing struggle to stay alive. Even cannibalism occurred. The best estimates are that 5 million people died. Yet the government, instead of helping, continued to take the grain. It used starvation to break resistance to collectivization in the Ukraine in what became the only man-made famine in history. Stalin called this policy "war by starvation."

Workers in industry were better off but not much. Although industry supposedly was being built according to an orderly plan, the furious pace Stalin demanded led to chaos and constant breakdowns. Virtually nothing was done to take care of the workers who were doing all of the building and producing. Khrushchev himself recalled the "unspeakable conditions—filth, bedbugs, cockroaches, bad food, inadequate clothing."³ In fact, he understated the situation. From housing to clothing to food, the workers had to do without. Overall, the standard of living during the worst years of the 1930s probably dropped by 50 percent, the most drastic decline in peacetime living conditions ever recorded. And when the workers complained about low pay, miserable working conditions, or high prices, as Khrushchev and many others recorded that they did, their complaints were met by harsh laws and savage punishments. Being twenty minutes late for work, for example, became a crime that could land a worker in prison.

There were some workers who were in no position to complain at all. These were the slave laborers in the huge network of labor camps run by the secret police. This network, known as the Gulag, became the largest slave-labor empire in history. Estimates are that between 8 and 15 million people labored in the Gulag during its peak years, and a large percentage of them died. They worked on all sorts of industrial and construction projects across the Soviet Union. Some of them toiled in and near Moscow, where Khrushchev was making his name.

In the middle of all this came the incredible episode known as the Great Purge. In a political sense the word *purge* usually refers to expelling people who have done something unacceptable from a party or government. Both Lenin and Stalin frequently made use of this type of punishment. But in the Soviet Union between 1934 and 1938 the word took on a new and terrible meaning. This purge destroyed millions of lives. Among its victims were nearly all of the old leaders who had been close to Lenin. Hundreds of thousands of loyal party workers, many of whom helped bring Stalin to power, were accused of crimes they could not possibly have committed and then were arrested. They included three quarters of those elected to the party's Central Committee in 1934, the year the purge started, and a majority of the country's military officer corps. Most were either shot outright or sent to their deaths in the camps.

Yet that was only a small part of the purge. Millions of innocent citizens outside the party were arrested and shipped to the labor camps, often to their deaths. The question of the era was simply "Why? What for?" These words were scratched into uncounted prison walls and transport vehicles by battered and bewildered victims. The answer, to the extent one exists at all, is complex. It begins with Stalin himself. Stalin wanted total and absolute power over the Soviet people and the Communist party. He got it as a result of the Great Purge. He unleashed a reign of terror that touched everyone. Nobody was secure, and the entire Soviet Union became subject to his whim.

But Stalin's motives, skills, and personal cruelty by themselves cannot explain how the Great Purge, or anything else that occurred during the 1930s, could have taken place. Whether the event in question is collectivization, the famine of 1932–33, or the Great Purge, it is important to understand that Stalin, who surely was guilty of unspeakable crimes, could not and did not act alone. His policies and crimes required the active support and participation of thousands of people. A key question therefore arises: How could ordinary people have done these things to each other?

Part of the answer is that the country passed through such terrible times both before and after 1917. World War I, the revolutions of 1917, and the Civil War uprooted millions of people and with them many traditional values and beliefs. Just to survive, many people became capable of doing things they would never have considered in normal times. In addition the Soviet people were subject to the steady drumbeat of a new morality. It insisted that anything that served the revolution was justified. Also, during events such as collectivization, industrialization, and the purges, there were careers to be made by people ruthless enough to seize the opportunity.

Years later, Khrushchev would attack a rival who had been head of the secret police because he made his career by "climbing over corpses." The point is that many did so. They collectivized the peasants without mercy, drove industrial workers without pause, and used slave laborers without guilt. They purged and arrested their colleagues without hesitation and then took their places on the next rung up the ladder. They justified their cruelty in various ways, often with the sincere conviction that they were building a better world. Among them, as hard, ruthless, and convinced of the rightness of the cause as any, was Nikita Sergeyevich Khrushchev.

Once in Moscow, Khrushchev began to rub shoulders with the Soviet Union's most powerful men, including those who were already close to Stalin and those who were on the way up. Khrushchev's transfer to Moscow and his placement on the fast track to the top owed much to the influence of Lazar Kaganovich. Although only a year older than Khrushchev, Kaganovich already had served as head of the Ukrainian Communist Party. He was now one of the secretaries of the Central Committee and about to become a member of the Politburo, the Soviet Union's most powerful political body. Even closer to Stalin was Vyacheslav Molotov, a Politburo member since 1926. He would hold some of the most important posts in the Soviet Union under Stalin. Also in Stalin's inner circle was Klimenty Voroshilov, a Civil War hero under whom Khrushchev had served but whose incompetence would lead to Soviet military disasters at the beginning of World War II.

Among those working their way up with Khrushchev were Nikolai Bulganin, Georgi Malenkov, and Nikolai Yezhov. Bulganin and Khrushchev would work closely together in Moscow under Stalin and for a few years after Stalin's death in 1953. Malenkov was destined to become one of Stalin's closest aides, only to lose the struggle for power with Khrushchev after 1953. Yezhov would disappear in 1938 but not before he served as head of the secret police and, as such, was Stalin's dreaded chief executioner during the peak years of the terror.

This was a fast crowd, but Khrushchev quickly proved that he could run with the best of them. Upon his arrival in Moscow in 1929 he was one of thousands of party members hoping to build a career. By 1934 he was on the Central Committee, making him one of the party's top one hundred officials. And in 1939, just after he left Moscow, Khrushchev became a full member of the Politburo, one of the dozen most powerful men in the entire Soviet Union.

Before he could do anything at the Stalin Industrial Academy, Khrushchev had to find a place to live. Housing was extremely scarce in Moscow, and Khrushchev had a wife and two children and was expecting a third child. He managed to find what he called an "ideal setup," a room within walking distance of his school.

Khrushchev's short, hectic career at the Industrial Academy—he attended only fifteen months and did not graduate— indicates that he was there to gain skills as a party enforcer, rather than to pick up any industrial managerial skills. Although Stalin had decisively won the struggle for power at the top, considerable opposition to him remained at the lower levels. One of those places was the Industrial Academy, where Nikolai

Bukharin, the last of Stalin's major rivals, had a following and where opposition to collectivization was strong. When the Bukharin forces managed to win an election at the academy in 1930, the results were voided and the school's party organization dissolved. A new election was quickly arranged and a new organization set up, with Khrushchev "elected" as its head, or secretary.

His first job was to purge the Bukharin supporters, or, as he put it, the "unstable and undesirable elements" who did "nothing but loaf."[4] One of the students most upset with collectivization was a young woman acquaintance of Khrushchev's named Nadezhda Alliluyeva. She also happened to be Stalin's wife. Alliluyeva, of course, was not purged. But she suffered terribly from what she knew was happening in the countryside and apparently did not hide her views from her husband. Eventually, her anguish became unbearable, and in 1932, as her friend Nikita Sergeyevich was enforcing Stalin's directives and rising in the ranks, she stunned everyone by committing suicide.

Khrushchev did his job at the academy well. In January 1931 he left the academy to take command of one of Moscow's district party organizations, the Bauman district. Khrushchev slipped comfortably into the shoes of the former leader, who had just been purged, the first of several times he would perform that maneuver.

Within six months Khrushchev took another step up. While retaining his post in the Bauman district, he was also given command of the largest and most important district in Moscow, the Red Presnya district. The man he was replacing had just been purged for an unforgivable offense: trying to ease the lives of the workers in his district by holding down prices in the stores where they bought food and clothing.

Khrushchev would commit no such blunder. Quite the opposite, he quickly demonstrated his mastery of what was called the "Stalin style of work." Simply put, this meant to drive workers as hard as possible. Comrade Khrushchev was an innovator in this area. He raised the quotas for what workers had to produce and lowered their wages. Workers were forceably recruited for specific jobs or made to work at an accelerated pace for a certain period of time, such as ten days. At the same time, they were made responsible for the machinery they worked on, a serious problem when it was impossible to find the time to maintain one's machines or tools. Khrushchev also vigorously enforced the harsh new decrees designed to control workers. These ranged from evicting workers from their homes for arriving late at work to putting their food ration cards, without which they could not survive, in the hands of their factory managers.

Nor was there much attention paid to feeding or housing people who were being worked so hard. The most Khrushchev seemed willing to do to increase inadequate food supplies was to work "zealously" to carry out Stalin's brainstorm that factories should raise rabbits for food. To this Khrushchev added his own clever idea: growing mushrooms in Moscow's cellars and ditches. In other words, if the overworked factory workers needed more food, they should raise it themselves in their almost nonexistent spare time.

Although Khrushchev naturally was doing all of this in order to keep his job and to get ahead, he had other motives as well. The 1930s were and still are viewed by the Soviet people as a period of heroic accomplishment. Khrushchev was a true believer in the idea that the party under the leadership of Stalin was building a better world. His memoirs, written when he had no need to mask his feelings, make this very clear:

> My comrades and I worked with enthusiasm and self-sacrifice. Our jobs consumed our whole lives. We knew no such thing as rest. We frequently called mass meetings or had consultations among ourselves on our days off, and we worked long hours, often well into the night. In our eyes there was something romantic about our task. Everyone lived to see the day when Lenin's words would come

*true: after the first ten years of its existence, Soviet Power would be invincible! Nowadays, unfortunately, a lot of that spirit of idealism and self-sacrifice has gone out of the Party. . . . Back when I helped run the city of Moscow, no one would have permitted himself so much as a single thought about having his own* dacha [*country house*]. *After all, we were Communists! [emphasis added]*[5]

A first-rate district party boss, Khrushchev soon moved up again. In February 1932 he was appointed Second Secretary of the Moscow Party Committee, the number-two man in Moscow. Actually, he was more than that. The First Secretary, Kaganovich, usually was busy with national matters, leaving Moscow to Khrushchev. Two years later this role became official when Khrushchev was made Moscow's First Secretary. Although official Soviet announcements are generally best treated skeptically, in this case it was both truthful and an excellent explanation of just why Khrushchev was doing so well:

*Comrade Khrushchev—a working man who has attended the school of struggle and of Party work, having started at the very bottom—is an outstanding representative of the post-October generation of Party workers, educated by Stalin. Under the guidance of that notable master of the Stalin method, Comrade Kaganovich, N. S. Khrushchev has grown step by step with our Party in recent years and is a worthy leader of our glorious Moscow Party organization.*[6]

The year 1934 was a big one for Khrushchev, as it was when he joined the party's Central Committee. It also was the year when the bulk of the work was done on one of the showpieces of the 1930s, a success closely associated with the name of Nikita Khrushchev—the subway system known as the Moscow Metro.

The building of the Moscow Metro tells a great deal about the Stalin regime and about Nikita Khrushchev. The Metro was hardly a necessity in 1930s Moscow. The city lacked not only modern conveniences but also many basic necessities, ranging from adequate housing to a proper sewage system. And the Metro certainly could have been built for much less money than it cost. But for Stalin and his associates it had to be built, and built to be the finest and fanciest in the world. It was, after all, to be a symbol of the future, and proof of the superiority of socialism, the Soviet Union, and, of course, Joseph Stalin.

The Metro cost over 500 million rubles, over 350 million in 1934 alone, the year most of it was completed. Meanwhile, the Soviet Union was spending only about 300 million rubles per year on consumer goods and producing only one shoe (*not* one pair of shoes) per person. It required 70,000 square meters of marble, over one-and-a-half times the total used in all of the tsarist palaces built during the monarchy's last fifty years. It absorbed the labor of more than seventy-five thousand workers, some of them forced laborers. Many of them never saw it finished because they died in accidents caused by the breakneck speed of construction that precluded adequate safety measures.

When it was completed—about a year late despite the rush—it was magnificent, truly "the most beautiful subway in the world," as a Soviet publicity brochure claimed. How could it be otherwise? The Moscow Metro was built with generous amounts of bronze, ceramic, and glazed panels, its interiors are graced with gold leaf, bas-relief, and mosaics, and several chandeliers. Perhaps the citizens of Moscow reasoned that not having shoes was not so bad since one could always ride the Metro.

Kaganovich was formally in charge of the construction, but in fact it was Khrushchev who supervised the work while Kaganovich was busy with other responsibilities. As usual, he threw himself into his work on the Metro, which absorbed 80 percent of his time. He seemed to be everywhere and involved in everything at once. After consulting with experts, he decided the method of tunneling had to be changed, and he got Stalin's approval to do so. He became involved in the design of the subway cars, rejecting the initial model in favor of another. He was directly involved in the decision to use an invention he had never heard of before—escalators—rather than elevators to move passengers to and from the surface.

Khrushchev also put on overalls and went down into the shafts to talk to the men digging the tunnels, inevitably urging them to go faster. Not even a trip to his office could distract him from his Metro; he often traveled there underground, via the tunnels his laborers were still digging!

Khrushchev's enthusiasm was matched only by his ruthlessness. There was no room for safety on this huge project. Tunnels were dug under buildings that often collapsed, proper precautions being taken only if foreigners lived in the structures above. Tunneling machinery was operated at several times the safe rate, with Khrushchev constantly urging workers to go still faster in the spirit of what was called "socialist competition." Laborers often worked several shifts in a row. Later, slave labor was employed to build several sections of the Metro. Floods, cave-ins, and other accidents took many lives. "The schedule grabbed us by the throat," Khrushchev's chief engineer recalled. In doing so, it often killed.

None of this got in Khrushchev's way. He drove the gigantic project to its conclusion. For that he earned his first major party award: the Order of the Red Banner of Labor.

Khrushchev chalked up other credits during these years. He was involved in the building of modern bakeries to replace the existing unsanitary ones. Other major projects included building a new reservoir for the city and cleaning up the polluted Moscow River. Khrushchev typically was on the spot for all of these projects, something that was none too pleasant when it came to the Moscow River:

*Before work began on the river, it had been a real cesspool into which human waste from all over Moscow was*

*dumped. I remember that Bulganin and I once inspected
the river in a police launch. The stench was so terrible that
we had to throw away our clothes afterwards.*[7]

Khrushchev's accomplishments boosted him up the party ladder. He was elected a delegate to the Seventeenth Party Congress. It met late in 1934, and Khrushchev received his first
opportunity to make a major speech at such an important
meeting. In 1935 he was promoted again. While keeping his
job as the First Secretary for the city of Moscow, he added the
post of First Secretary for the Moscow region, the large territory
surrounding the capital. He also was made a candidate, or
nonvoting, member of the Politburo.

Agriculture was another area that drew Khrushchev's attention. He was not directly involved in collectivization during
the worst years of the early 1930s although he certainly knew
what was going on. In his memoirs he recalled, among other
episodes about collectivization, a "business trip" Kaganovich
made in 1932. It was to deal with what the Soviets called
"sabotage," or resistance to collectivization. Kaganovich ended
the "sabotage" by deporting entire villages to Siberia. Khrushchev also participated directly in collectivization in the
Moscow region. In his memoirs Khrushchev recognized some of
the catastrophic results of collectivization, admitting that the
"Stalin brand of collectivization brought us nothing but misery
and brutality." He then defended the political opponents Stalin
blamed for the trouble, putting the blame "squarely on Stalin's
own shoulders." Khrushchev did not look any further, beyond
Stalin to the commissars like himself who supported Stalin
so completely and who so eagerly carried out his orders. The
best Khrushchev can say is that they "believed in Stalin and
trusted him."[8]

In those days Khrushchev's faith in Stalin was complete. In
his memoirs, written long after he had denounced Stalin for all
sorts of crimes, Khrushchev not only admits that he idolized

Stalin but insists that Stalin accomplished a great deal despite his errors and crimes. Perhaps this helps explain how Khrushchev was able to go overboard in praising Stalin in the 1930s and 1940s. Certainly, no one did it better, not even Kaganovich, whom Khrushchev would later call Stalin's "lackey." Khrushchev's public speeches are littered with adoring praise of Stalin. For Khrushchev, Stalin was the Soviet Union's "teacher and *vozhd* [leader]," its "*vozhd* of genius." Stalin was "hope, he is expectation; he is the beacon that guides all progressive mankind." Stalin was also the nation's "banner," its "will," and its "victory."9

All of this was a great help to Stalin in consolidating and building his power. At the same time, there is no doubt that it helped Khrushchev. While faith and sincerity certainly played a role in Khrushchev's adoration of Stalin, personal interest and career advancement played at least as large a role. The ability to combine faith and career, after all, was in many ways the essence of Nikita Khrushchev.

The ultimate test of Khrushchev's ability to prosper in Stalin's Russia began late in 1934 with the onset of the Great Purge. It began with the murder of Sergei Kirov, the party boss in Leningrad and one of the top party leaders nationally. Khrushchev and others have accused Stalin of responsibility for Kirov's murder, and with good reason. Aside from Stalin, Kirov was the most popular party leader. By 1934 he also was associated with those in the party who believed the time had come to ease up. Collectivization was accomplished and the First Five-Year Plan (1929–34) completed. There was also the feeling that some of the people defeated in the political struggles of the 1920s could now be forgiven and readmitted to the party.

Stalin opposed these ideas. While it is uncertain exactly what he believed, it is safe to say that any relaxation in tensions at home would have limited his drive toward absolute power. Perhaps Kirov's popularity was enough to worry Stalin into acting, regardless of what Kirov happened to think about any given issue. At any rate, in December 1934 Kirov was assassinated. The murder ignited a firestorm that burned its way through the party and country for over three years at a cost of millions of lives.

After he came to power, and again after he fell and went into retirement, Khrushchev condemned Stalin for many of the crimes committed during the Great Purge. His memoirs are filled with references to murdered party members, whom he remembered as "loyal," "good Communists," and "honest." During the purges it was another story.

Khrushchev may not have been in the inner circle that directed the purge with Stalin. This circle included Malenkov, Molotov, Kaganovich, and the two secret police chiefs between 1934 and 1938, Genrikh Yagoda and Nikolai Yezhov. But Khrushchev was close enough. He was one of a select group that directly investigated the Kirov murder. He also had close ties to Kaganovich and to both Yagoda and Yezhov.

Moreover, like these men, Khrushchev had something to lose if Kirov's ideas were followed. They had advanced up the ladder as Stalin's toughs. An easing of tensions would have slowed their advance. Even worse, men like Khrushchev would probably have been weakened by the return to the party of men they had replaced, men who often were very competent and had party roots going back to Lenin's day. Instead, the purges opened up new opportunities for the meanest and craftiest, as Khrushchev's rapid rise during those years testifies.

It is not surprising that Khrushchev was one of the most vocal and vicious supporters of the Great Purge. He denounced all "enemies of the people." It was essential, he warned, to "draw our proletarian sword to chop off the heads of the loathsome creatures, double dealers, and murderers, agents of fascism. . . ." He urged vigilance against "the scum of the smashed exploiting classes . . . these spies . . . and murderers."[10]

Who were these "loathsome creatures," these "spies," "murderers," and "scum of the smashed exploiting classes"?

They were every member of Lenin's politburo, the men who had made the revolution in the first place and who had lived into the 1930s. They were two thirds of the delegates to the recent Seventeenth Party Congress to whom Khrushchev had spoken so respectfully. They were most of the Soviet Union's top military commanders and half of the Red Army's entire officer corps. They were also thousands of the country's artists and scientists, hundreds of thousands of party members, and millions of honest, hardworking Soviet citizens. Years later Khrushchev would devote many pages in his memoirs to expressing regret and anger at the number of "good Communists" who died during the purges. He devoted no space at all to his responsibility for those deaths.

Late in 1938 Stalin ended the Great Purge. It had become so destructive that it threatened the country's stability. Yezhov was arrested and disappeared. The new secret police chief, Lavrenti Beria, continued to arrest people but at a slower, more controlled pace. Meanwhile, Khrushchev had been given another assignment. In January 1938 he left Moscow to return to the Ukraine as First Secretary of the Ukrainian Communist party. The fitter from Yuzovka had become the ruler of the Ukraine, a region of 35 million people.

Khrushchev took the place of the purged Stanislav Kosior, the man who had headed the Ukraine when Nikita had left back in 1929. During this last year of the Great Purge, Khrushchev's first assignment quite naturally was to purge the Ukrainian party. He proved to be as good at this as any of his Moscow colleagues. Within half a year he had eliminated most of the Ukrainian Central Committee. And he was only getting warmed up. By 1940 more than half of the people he had promoted when he arrived had been replaced. No wonder the local secret police chief, a man in a position to know, commented that "only after the faithful Stalinist, Nikita Sergeyevich Khrushchev, arrived in the Ukraine did the smashing of the enemies of the people begin in earnest."[11] Part of the

*Joseph Stalin (left) visits the*
*forty-three-year-old Nikita Khrushchev*
*in the Ukraine in 1937.*

reason for such a thorough purge was the fear in Moscow of Ukrainian nationalism. It was no secret that the Ukraine resented Russian domination. Stalin feared that the Ukraine, located on the Soviet Union's western border, might someday be tempted to use foreign help to break away from the Soviet Union. Therefore, Khrushchev was given the job of suppressing Ukrainian national feeling and culture. His tactics included arresting local intellectuals, rewriting the history books, and stressing Russian in the schools at the expense of Ukrainian. For this he earned Stalin's praise. Many others saw things differently; they called him the "butcher of the Ukraine."

Khrushchev's assignment required that he do much more than purge and suppress. He had to expand the Ukrainian economy, which was still suffering from the effects of collectivization and the purges. In this he was quite successful. The Ukraine exceeded its planned targets in both agriculture and industry. Khrushchev's efforts in this area were as important to him as they were to the Ukraine. They allowed him to test and develop his unique political style on a grand scale. His work also gave him vast experience in governing in general and considerable knowledge (although not nearly as much as he thought) of agriculture in particular. As he had done in Yuzovka and Moscow, Khrushchev traveled right to the source: to the factories, the mines, and especially the collective farms. As his efforts produced respectable results, he began to earn a national reputation as an agricultural expert.

Yet soon Khrushchev would be distracted by other concerns. As the harvest of 1939 was ripening, armies were preparing to turn grainfields into battlefields. September had arrived and with it the start of World War II.

# FOUR

# WAR, RECONSTRUCTION, AND DEATH THROES

When the German army marched into Poland on September 1, 1939, and most of Europe went to war, the Soviet Union remained at peace. This was because of the agreement Stalin and Hitler had signed eight days earlier. In a treaty that shocked the Western powers, Nazi Germany and Soviet Russia, supposedly archenemies, publicly agreed on a nonaggression pact. In a secret addition to that pact, the two powers divided up Poland and the rest of Eastern Europe between themselves.

By freeing Hitler from any fear of a Soviet attack from the east, Stalin allowed Germany to wage war with the rest of Europe. For two years, until Hitler double-crossed his partner in the Kremlin, the Soviet Union was in many ways Germany's most valuable ally. It provided Hitler with diplomatic support, naval bases, and many of the raw materials the Nazi war machine needed. No wonder that Hitler called Stalin "indispensable" and "a hell of a fellow."

What Stalin's fellow Communists called him, at least in private, is not known. Most of them, even high-ranking officials like Khrushchev, were told nothing until the pact was announced. It certainly came as a shock. For years Soviet propaganda had portrayed fascism in general and Germany in particular as dire threats to their country. Khrushchev later recalled that he and his colleagues were so stunned that they could not even discuss it among themselves, much less explain it to the population at large.

The Soviets moved quickly to take over the Polish territory promised them in the Nazi-Soviet pact. In the middle of September the Red Army invaded eastern Poland, an area the Soviets preferred to call the western Ukraine. Right behind the army came party officials, whose task it was to crush any resistance and to attach the region to the Soviet Union. Nikita Khrushchev, the party boss of the Ukraine, was the man in charge of this pitiless job, a process the Russians blandly called "sovietization."

Sovietization had several facets. Although Khrushchev claimed he was engaged in "liberating" a population that was "jubilant" at his arrival, in fact he was prepared for a very different reaction. The region, after all, was not populated by Russians but by other nationalities: mainly Ukrainians but also many Poles and Jews. It was now covered by a virtual avalanche of propaganda material. This included tons of Soviet newspapers, 800,000 portraits of Soviet leaders, and 3.5 *million* brochures and leaflets. Entertainers and artists were imported from the Soviet Ukraine to demonstrate the joys of life in the Soviet Union.

To persuade the unconvinced, the secret police swung into action. They immediately began arresting tens of thousands of people. Those with the potential for any independence at all—business people, clergy, intellectuals, community leaders, members of any kind of political party—were shot or deported to Soviet labor camps. One of Khrushchev's major concerns was the depth of Ukrainian nationalism. It was a problem he knew well from the Soviet Ukraine, and it was even stronger in the territory just taken from Poland. He was also concerned with the thousands of dazed Polish troops retreating eastward toward Soviet-occupied territory after being overwhelmed by the German army. Instead of finding shelter, they were rounded up and deported with the civilians. Altogether, the total number of deportees topped 1 million. Very few lived to return to their homes after the war.

Meanwhile, Khrushchev was preparing "elections." Not surprisingly, Communist candidates won close to 100 percent of the votes and immediately elected to annex the western Ukraine to the Soviet Union. Khrushchev then turned to collectivization, which he carried out without delay or mercy. He had good reason to work fast. In 1940 he was doing everything all over again, this time in a region called Bessarabia, just seized from Rumania. In the north his associates were doing the same thing in the Baltic countries of Lithuania, Latvia, and Estonia.

As Khrushchev and his colleagues worked feverishly to absorb these new territories into the Soviet Union, time was running out. The purges had left the Soviet army in terrible shape. This was convincingly demonstrated in 1940, when the Soviet Union attacked Finland. The Soviets were trying to enforce their demand that the Finns cede them some strategically important territory. Although the Red Army eventually won the war, the tiny Finnish army first scored many victories. The Soviet Union was humiliated. Over two hundred thousand of its soldiers died before the Red Army finally defeated the Finns.

After that, Stalin worked hard to improve the Soviet military but with limited success. Too many of his best officers were dead or in prison. Reorganization also suffered because Stalin tried to control everything himself. For example, in 1941 he instructed Khrushchev to investigate the possibilities of mounting a certain type of diesel engine on airplanes. Where was Khrushchev to find the engines? Stalin told him a large factory in the Ukrainian city of Kharkov made them. Yet Khrushchev, the man in charge of the Ukraine, knew nothing about that vital factory.

Another problem was that Stalin, although he feared Hitler and expected a German invasion someday, hoped to delay war with Germany as long as possible. Therefore, he did little to improve the readiness of troops on the Soviet Union's western border, the very troops who would have to face the Germans first when they invaded. So determined was Stalin to avoid war that when information began to arrive that the Germans were preparing for war, he chose to ignore it. In the end Stalin was told the exact day of the German invasion from more than one source.

One such source was Khrushchev, whose responsibilities in the Ukraine included a large part of the front facing the Germans. During the night of June 21–22, 1941, a German soldier crossed over to the Soviet side with the news that the invasion would occur the next morning. Khrushchev and Georgi Zhukov, the general in charge of the Ukrainian front, who would later become the Soviet Union's greatest war hero, phoned Stalin. The dictator ignored their warning. Khrushchev endured a sleepless night. The next morning, June 22, the Germans came in full force. Stalin, still hoping to avoid war, gave the order not to shoot back! It was no use. War had begun.

World War II, the Soviet Union's "Great Patriotic War," was a desperate struggle for survival. Millions of Soviet citizens, especially in Khrushchev's Ukraine but also elsewhere, welcomed the German armies as liberators from a system and regime they hated. The incompetence of many of Stalin's cronies who occupied key military positions cost the Soviet Union many battles and millions of casualties. Even as the battles raged, the slave-labor camps continued to hold millions of men who could have been fighting the Germans, and the secret police continued to arrest even more. During the early days of the war Stalin suffered what amounted to a nervous breakdown. He was unable to speak to his anxious people on the radio until July 3, fully eleven days after the German invasion.

In the meantime the Germans advanced. They overwhelmed Soviet forces, taking huge numbers of prisoners and terrorizing civilians. The Nazis also began their merciless slaughter of Jews, who, because of Stalin's attempt to maintain good relations with Hitler, had had no warning about the Nazis' attitude toward them or of the invasion itself. The years 1941 and 1942 brought almost uninterrupted disaster, although the Germans were stopped at the gates of Leningrad and Moscow, the Soviet Union's two major cities. Only in early 1943, with the help of massive military supplies from the United States and the other Allies, did the tide begin to turn. It then took two more years of bitter fighting for the Soviet Union, the United States, and the rest of the Allies to defeat the Germans. By the time World War II was over, much of the western part of the Soviet Union lay in ruins. At least 20 million Soviet citizens were dead.

Khrushchev was in the thick of the battle, from the disastrous defeats to the great victories. Once again he was a political commissar, although in this war his responsibility was for entire armies, not just for a small unit. His experiences at the front distinguished him from most other top party leaders. Almost all of them spent the war far from the guns and the dying. This is important, for it seems that the war changed Khrushchev. The early disasters were a blinding floodlight shining directly on Stalin's incompetence and mistakes. They also moved Khrushchev to disagree with Stalin for the first time. Suddenly Stalin was a human being, not a superman; a blunderer, not a genius; a man who knew fear, and not, as his name meant in Russian, the "man of steel."

Equally important, the war brought Khrushchev face to face with the great suffering and courage of the Soviet people. He was the horrified witness to the mass desertions and defections to the enemy when the Germans swept into the Ukraine. He also was there when the Red Army made its incredible stand at Stalingrad. All of this seems to have had its effect. When he came to power years later, Khrushchev understood that the Soviet system could no longer treat the people as it had under

Stalin. The people's needs, not only the need to build communism, therefore became a priority once Khrushchev became the leader of the Soviet Union.

But first Khrushchev had to survive the war, something that seemed unlikely during its early days. Aside from the Germans, Khrushchev found himself dealing with incompetence and despair. Shortly after the German attack in 1941, he phoned Moscow with a desperate request for rifles. His conversation with Malenkov left him stunned:

> "Tell me . . . where can we get rifles? . . ."
>
> "You'd better give up any thought of getting rifles. The rifles here . . . have all been sent to Leningrad."
>
> "Then what are we supposed to fight with?"
>
> "I don't know—pikes, swords, homemade weapons, anything you can make in your factories."
>
> "You mean we should fight tanks with spears?"
>
> "You'll have to do the best you can. You can make fire bombs out of bottles of gasoline or kerosene and throw them at the tanks."[1]

That conversation was followed a few days later by one that was even worse. One of Khrushchev's generals came to him and told him the situation was hopeless. Before Khrushchev could do anything, the officer "drew his pistol and shot himself, right there in front of me."[2]

By then Kiev, the Ukrainian capital, was virtually surrounded. Stalin insisted that there should be no retreat, an order that threatened hundreds of thousands of troops with destruction. Khrushchev then took the initiative, a very risky step for anyone close to Stalin. He ordered a retreat on his own. His commanding general at the front hesitated because Khrushchev's orders contradicted Stalin's. By the time the general acted, it was too late. Huge numbers of troops were lost. Kiev fell to the Germans.

The only ray of success in all of this gloom of failure occurred during the retreat from Kharkov, the Ukraine's second largest city. Khrushchev remained at his command post until the last moment to make sure the Germans would not suspect anything. Meanwhile he had it mined. Just after he escaped by plane, the Germans took Kharkov and settled in at Khrushchev's former command post. When the command post blew up, the explosion killed many German officers, including the commanding general of the entire Kharkov campaign.

The next year, 1942, brought more disaster. Khrushchev was deeply involved in an offensive launched to retake Kharkov. After some advances it became clear that the Soviet troops were moving into a trap. Again Khrushchev called Stalin, again advising a retreat, and again Stalin refused. Khrushchev later claimed that he fought hard to change Stalin's mind. But eyewitnesses reported that after that phone conversation Khrushchev carried out Stalin's orders with a vengeance. He told one general who continued to urge a retreat:

> I myself, with my own hands, will blow out your brains. I'll shoot you to death like the lowest dog. I'll finish you off as the lowest scum of the earth! I order you: continue the offensive![3]

Ten days later, his army destroyed, the general phoned Khrushchev to inform him of the disaster. He added he was carrying out Khrushchev's threatened sentence himself. He then committed suicide, as did his top aide.

After the Kharkov disaster the tide of battle gradually changed. The key battle took place in Stalingrad, a city in southern Russia on the Volga River. Here the Red Army fought with its back to the river against the full fury of the German army. The battle raged for months. The fighting went street by

*Residents of Stalingrad (today Volgograd)
return to their destroyed homes in 1943 after
the city was bombed by the Germans.*

street, house to house, inch by inch, hand to hand. It was a savage struggle in which the Russian soldiers simply refused to break. The Red Army won the respect of the world in what was probably its finest hour.

Stalingrad was also Khrushchev's finest wartime hour. He was all over the front lines, maintaining discipline, restoring morale, solving problems. He participated in planning the offensive in early 1943 that brought his country its greatest victory of the war. A few months later he was at Kursk, very close to where he was born, for the greatest tank battle of the war. The advancing Germans were thrown back, to begin their long, bitter, bloody retreat to Berlin.

After Kursk and during the last two years of the war, as the victories mounted, Khrushchev won several promotions and medals. But in fact the fighting was largely over for him by 1944. Once Kiev was retaken in November 1943—Khrushchev reported to Stalin the devastated place was "like a city of the dead"—his main job was to rebuild the Soviet governing structure and restore the economy of the Ukraine. Amid chaos and desolation, and with his usual energy and ruthlessness, he began a task that lasted well beyond the end of the war.

To do the job Khrushchev was given unprecedented authority. Together with his post as First Secretary of the Ukrainian Communist party, Stalin appointed Khrushchev head of the Ukrainian government as well. The destruction in parts of the Ukraine was almost total. Millions of people lived in dugouts, holes dug into the earth and covered with whatever was available. Until the war ended in 1945, there were no able-bodied men to help rebuild, only, as Khrushchev put it, "old men, invalids, those unfit for military service, and particularly the women."4

In addition to these problems, many Ukrainians especially in the regions annexed in 1939, did not welcome Khrushchev back. They hated the party and Russian control of their country. They organized themselves into guerrilla bands that fought the returning Russian Communists during the remainder of the war and for several years thereafter.

There is considerable controversy surrounding these Ukrainian opponents of Soviet rule. Many of them, as the Soviets claim, had cooperated with the Nazi occupiers during the war. They willingly and cruelly participated in the German-organized systematic extermination of Jews between 1941 and 1945. They were murderous criminals by any standard and deserved to be treated as such. At the same time there were other Ukrainians who had fought the Germans as foreign occupiers. After November 1943 they opposed the returning agents of Moscow for the same reason. Stalin, Khrushchev, and the party, of course, did not bother with this distinction nor any other. To them anybody who suggested that the Ukraine had the right to determine its own future was an "enemy of the people" and had to be destroyed.

The Ukrainian rebels were strengthened by unpopular Soviet policies. First among them was the reestablishment of the collective farms. The peasants had dissolved them during the war after Soviet forces were driven from the region. Now Khrushchev and the party were restoring the hated collectives. People were also infuriated when prisoners of war and those who had been forced laborers in Germany were treated like traitors and arrested. The full force of the Red Army and armed units of the secret police had to be used against the rebels until, after great bloodshed, they were wiped out.

Against this background Khrushchev struggled to restore the Ukrainian economy. The end of the war in 1945 should have improved matters. But 1946 brought a severe drought and a very poor harvest. Although Khrushchev continued to be Stalin's enforcer, this time he did something he had never done before. Nikita Khrushchev appealed to Stalin to help feed the Ukraine.

The request was denied. Once again the state took all of the available grain, and once again there was famine. And again there was cannibalism. From his officials in the field Khrushchev received reports of horrid scenes. Yet there was little he could do. And to make matters worse, he soon found that he was in trouble himself.

In March 1947 Khrushchev was suddenly replaced as head of the Ukrainian government. In his place Stalin put Lazar Kaganovich, his number-one troubleshooter and enforcer. Khrushchev also had to give up several of his other positions, although he officially remained as First Secretary of the Ukrainian Communist Party. For six months Khrushchev remained out of sight.

It is still unclear exactly what happened. Khrushchev certainly suffered a demotion, a fate that was always dangerous and often fatal in Stalin's Russia. The probable cause of his troubles was that since the Soviet reoccupation of the Ukraine Khrushchev had not been tough enough for his boss in Moscow. One possible sign of his weakness was his appeal to Stalin for food in 1946. A more certain failing was the pace of recollectivization. Under Khrushchev during 1944 to 1946 only about five hundred collectives were reestablished. In only six months Kaganovich established over fifteen hundred.

Another problem was that Khrushchev seems not to have been harsh enough in dealing with Ukrainian national feeling. This was a particularly serious defect since in 1946 the Soviet government began a thorough and deadly campaign against what it considered foreign influences. Thousands of people of all kinds were arrested. Their crimes often were nothing more than reading foreign literature or listening to the wrong music. One particularly vicious aspect of this campaign was an outburst of anti-Semitism that resulted in the execution of many cultural and artistic leaders of the Jewish community.

One other factor may have contributed to Khrushchev's decline. He reports in his memoirs that he had a severe case of pneumonia. Apparently he barely survived and was in bed for months. In the end, however, Khrushchev survived both physically and politically. In December 1947 Kaganovich left his job in the Ukraine and returned to Moscow. Khrushchev surfaced as his replacement.

The next two years were successful ones. Khrushchev was a tiger on the cultural front against Ukrainian nationalism and ethnic identity. The economy did very well in 1948 and 1949, in both agriculture and industry. In 1948 Khrushchev was awarded the Order of Lenin for his work.

In the meantime the political waters were churning in Moscow. One of the top party leaders, Andrei Zhdanov, died mysteriously in August 1948. Stalin then launched a new purge. Its toll quickly ran into the thousands. Georgi Malenkov, Zhdanov's main rival for Stalin's favor at the time, was running the purge, which is now known as the "Leningrad Affair." At this point Stalin decided to bring Khrushchev to Moscow, probably to offset Malenkov's growing power. Khrushchev was appointed First Secretary for both Moscow city and province. In addition, he was made one of the secretaries of the Central Committee, a very powerful position.

Moscow was an uncomfortable and dangerous place when Khrushchev arrived for his second tour of duty there. In fact, Khrushchev was very concerned when he received notification to report to Moscow immediately. He knew that one of Stalin's techniques was to call officials to Moscow for one reason or another and then have them arrested. His mind was eased when he received a phone call from Malenkov just before his departure from Kiev, telling him he had nothing to fear. Khrushchev, who would have little good to say about Malenkov in over eleven hundred pages of memoirs, remembers that in this case he was "genuinely touched" by Malenkov's gesture. 5

In Moscow the aftereffects of the Leningrad Affair still lingered. In 1950 the Korean War broke out. The heightened Soviet-American tensions resulting from this war frayed many nerves, especially Stalin's. Meanwhile, his top lieutenants schemed and maneuvered. Malenkov, master of intrigue and manipulator of the party machine, kept an eye on everyone. Aside from Stalin, his major concern was Khrushchev. The man from the Ukraine had accumulated considerable power. He had built a loyal political network during his years in the Ukraine. He had many powerful friends in the military dating from his war service. With his transfer to Moscow and his powerful new posts, Khrushchev had emerged, along with Malenkov, as one of the two strongest men in the Soviet Union after Stalin.

This was particularly important because by this time Stalin was clearly declining. Life was never easy around Stalin. He was always suspicious, vicious, and given to paranoia. His working hours stretched deep into the night and often included long feasts and drinking bouts. This took its toll on his top lieutenants, who had to endure these all-night sessions and then be ready for a normal working day. But in the years after 1949 things became even worse. Stalin would stare at those around him and ask, "Why are your eyes so shifty?" He increasingly enjoyed humiliating his top aides. Once he made Khrushchev, a man in his mid-fifties, dance the *gopak*, a dance that requires getting down on one's haunches and kicking out one's heels. The dinners became, as Khrushchev put it, "sheer torture." He and the others had to taste Stalin's food first to make sure it was not poisoned. When he was alone, the aging dictator lived in his quarters in the Kremlin behind armored doors. His trips to his country houses were in armored cars, by routes he chose personally at the last moment. In this atmosphere of gloom and fear the government, Khrushchev claims, "virtually ceased to function."[6]

Not even these conditions kept Khrushchev from being Khrushchev. He now considered himself something of an agricultural expert. A tour in 1950 of the collective farms around Moscow spurred him into action. Khrushchev felt that these farms, long neglected and poverty-stricken, were too small to be efficient. His strategy was to combine them. Within a year their number had dropped from six thousand to fifteen hundred.

Ultimately, Khrushchev's goal was to create what he called "agrotowns." These would be large modern towns that would replace peasant villages and offer the farmers all of the comforts and cultural advantages of the cities.

The plan to combine the collectives was reasonably successful. Many of them began to do better. But Khrushchev ran into trouble in 1951 when he tried a pilot "agrotown" project. It was mismanaged from the start. A number of peasants from several villages were forced to move from their homes to another village. They then had to pay the moving costs themselves. Some party officials began to criticize the project. Stalin then turned against it, and it was scrapped. This failure also gave Malenkov a chance to criticize Khrushchev publicly.

The next round in the Khrushchev-Malenkov rivalry took place at the Nineteenth Party Congress in 1952. This was a major event, as there had been no congress for thirteen years. Because he lacked the strength, for the first time since the 1920s Stalin did not give the main report. That honor went to Malenkov. However, Khrushchev was still very much in the picture. He gave the important report on party rules.

Although he stayed in the background, Stalin still made the main news at the congress. To the dismay of his top aides he announced that the nine-man Politburo would be replaced by a twenty-five-man Presidium. Stalin's intent clearly was to dilute the power of *all* of his top men. Having accomplished this, what he intended to do was uncertain. What *is* certain is that Stalin's action was a total, chilling surprise.

On the heels of the Nineteenth Congress came the bizarre "Doctors' Plot." Stalin, whose anti-Semitism was no secret, claimed that he had uncovered a plot by a group of doctors, most of them Jewish, to murder top party officials. Aside from what evil this boded for the Soviet Union's Jewish population, this new Stalin nightmare threatened many if not all of his top aides. They feared his increasing paranoia and knew full well that once a purge was unleashed it could go in any direction.

This time, however, with the exception of two of the

accused doctors who died in prison, everyone survived. On the night of March 1–2, 1953, Stalin suffered a stroke. The man who normally had the best of everything the Soviet Union had to offer could not be treated by his personal physician. He was in prison because of the "Doctors' Plot." The stricken dictator's top aides now gathered around to see what would happen. Khrushchev and fellow Presidium member Nikolai Bulganin kept watch on the sick man around the clock.

Fear was everywhere as Stalin's top lieutenants awaited his death. They dreaded Stalin but had no idea how they would get along without him. They feared each other but knew they had to work together when Stalin died. Khrushchev himself records that he genuinely felt sorry for Stalin and actually shed tears for the man he still, through it all, deeply respected.

On March 5, 1953, the curtain finally rang down on the Stalin era—but not before one last scene, filled with all of the foreboding and terror that had marked the past quarter century. Stalin's daughter Svetlana remembers her father's final exit:

> At what seemed like the very last moment he suddenly opened his eyes and cast a glance over everyone in the room. It was a terrible glance. . . . The glance swept over everyone in a second. Then something incomprehensible and awesome happened that to this day I can't understand. He suddenly lifted his left hand as though he were pointing to something above and bringing down a curse on us all. The gesture was incomprehensible and full of menace, and no one could say to whom or what it might be directed. The next moment, the spirit wrenched itself free of the flesh. 7

For Stalin's former assistants, a new act in the great Soviet drama was beginning. For one of them, Nikita S. Khrushchev, once an extra, then a bit player, later a major supporting actor, the time was finally approaching to move to center stage.

# FIVE
# SUCCESS AND DESTALINIZATION

Although Stalin's death was welcome news to many, it also caused sadness, uncertainty, and fear in the Soviet Union. Stalin's death was welcomed because life under him had been unbearably harsh. Ordinary citizens endured a miserably low standard of living. They also lived with waves of terror that suddenly came and went. Those at the top lived much better, sometimes quite luxuriously. Yet they lived with the unnerving knowledge that they, too, could lose everything in a single stroke in a new purge. This fear reached even into the Kremlin and to the men immediately around Stalin, especially during the dictator's last years.

At the same time, Stalin was also missed. Over two decades of unending propaganda had done its work. Millions of average Soviet citizens believed in Comrade Stalin's greatness and loved him. Now they mourned his death and wondered what would become of their country without its great leader. Those at the top knew Stalin better, but they had the same fear. They had depended on Stalin for their entire political lives. Now they had to manage by themselves. Stalin's passing left a huge gap in Soviet political life. Suddenly and unprepared, Khrushchev, Malenkov, Molotov, Beria, and the rest of the Soviet leadership had to enter that dark and dangerous unknown.

What made this so frightening was the combination of tasks and threats these men faced. Their personal security demanded that Stalin's murderous methods of dealing with the party be abolished. It required that nobody be permitted to accumulate the power Stalin once held. Meanwhile, Stalin's successors had to keep the country calm and maintain stability. They shared a general consensus that this meant introducing reforms to make life better for the mass of the people. Life could not continue as it was under Stalin—in terms of either the low standard of living or the harsh repression of the previous twenty years—because of the risk of popular revolt. This fact was driven home by a series of revolts in many of the Gulag labor camps during 1953 and 1954. The worst of them lasted for forty-two days during the spring and summer of 1954. It required three thousand troops backed by tanks to finally put it down.

The Soviet Union's new rulers also had to do something to reduce international tensions, which had risen to dangerous levels during the ongoing Korean War. And while dealing with all of this, they had to watch each other as they schemed and struggled against one another for survival and power.

Whatever their fears and uncertainties, Stalin's former lieutenants moved very quickly as soon as he was dead. Their first job was to restore the power they had lost during Stalin's last months. On March 6, 1953, Moscow was ringed by Beria's secret police troops, armed with tanks and flame throwers. At a meeting in the Kremlin the top party and government posts were distributed. Malenkov received the top jobs and, it appeared, the most power. He was made both prime minister of the country and senior secretary of the party's Central Committee. Behind him was Lavrenty Beria, Stalin's long-time secret police chief. Along with the tremendous power he held as head of the secret police, Beria added the posts of Minister of Interior and first deputy prime minister. Molotov became foreign minister and, like Beria, a first deputy prime minister.

Khrushchev ranked just behind these three, although in reality he was more powerful than Molotov. However, his power was not as visible as was that of his colleagues. This was primarily because Khrushchev did not head a governmental ministry and actually gave up one important party post, his position as First Secretary of the Moscow region. But the peasant from Kalinovka emerged as the Central Committee secretary responsible for overseeing the powerful party Secretariat. This gave him greater influence over party jobs and appointments than any other leader. Khrushchev also took charge of arranging the late dictator's funeral. Stalin's henchmen then purged the party Presidium of the new men Stalin had brought in only months before and proclaimed their ranks were "united and unshakable."

Cracks quickly appeared in these ranks anyway. On March 14 Malenkov's colleagues forced him to give up his post as senior party secretary. They did not want him, or anybody else, to accumulate too much power and become another Stalin. That important job went to Khrushchev, possibly because the three senior men did not consider him a serious candidate for supreme power. The other possibility is that Khrushchev played the leading role in downgrading Malenkov and accordingly took the senior secretary post as his part of the spoils.

In any case, Khrushchev played the risky political game brilliantly. A man generally known for his rashness and impatience, Khrushchev remained calm and patient. He used his job as senior secretary—he was officially designated First Secretary in September—to move his supporters into key party positions. At the same time he plotted against Beria, whose control of the secret police made him a threat to everyone else.

Moving against Beria was especially dangerous. Secret police spies were everywhere. Khrushchev also could never be sure his partners in the plot would not betray him. One major concern was Malenkov, who feared Beria but was also his good friend. Khrushchev initially did not even know how to arrest Beria. After all, Beria controlled the secret police and the Kremlin guards. This forced Khrushchev to bring the military into the plot. The key man here was Marshal Georgi Zhukov, the great war hero and deputy defense minister.

The trap was sprung in July at a Kremlin meeting. Zhukov's army troops moved into position in the Kremlin and at key secret police centers around Moscow. Beria was arrested but not before the incredible tension led to a situation that was almost as comical as it was frightening. As Khrushchev recalls it:

> *When everyone had spoken, Malenkov . . . was supposed to sum things up and to formulate a consensus, but at the last moment he lost his nerve. After the final speech, the session was left hanging. There was a long pause. I saw we were in trouble, so I asked . . . for the floor in order to propose a motion . . . [to strip Beria of his posts]. . . . Malenkov was still in a state of panic. As I recall, he didn't even put my motion to a vote. He pressed a secret button which gave the signal to the generals who were waiting in the next room. . . .* [1]

Elsewhere in Moscow many of Beria's top aides were being arrested, while others were shot to death right in their offices. Beria's trial came in December. At first he was confident. He greeted one witness against him by asking: "What, are you still alive?"[2] But when the sentence was pronounced the man who had sent so many to their deaths broke. He wept and begged for mercy. His pleas, like millions of others, were in vain. Beria was executed immediately.

His fall marked much more than the end of one man's political career or life. It marked the end of the independent power of the secret police, from which no Soviet citizen, not even top party officials, was safe. Before 1953 the secret police had served one leader—Stalin. He had used them as a weapon against all of the others. After Beria's fall the secret police became responsible to the party leadership as a whole. No longer could one contender for power use them against his rivals. This meant that methods other than violence and terror would have to be used in any political struggle. It also meant that new methods would have to be found to govern the country. This was a momentous change, in effect the most important single reform of the post-Stalin era.

Beria's removal was followed by a drawn-out showdown between Malenkov and Khrushchev. At first Malenkov appeared stronger. Then he made several errors. His attempt to hold the top party and government posts made many of his colleagues fear him. He further damaged himself with promises designed to win public support. Malenkov pledged to raise the Soviet standard of living immediately. His strategy was to produce more consumer goods for the people and spend more to produce food by cutting back on heavy industry. This angered powerful party leaders in charge of heavy industry as well as military leaders who depended on them for armaments.

Khrushchev meanwhile positioned himself well. He attacked Malenkov's proposals as dangerous. This won him friends among leaders in heavy industry and the military. As First Secretary he continued to place his supporters in key positions. While Malenkov remained in Moscow and plotted, as he had under Stalin, Khrushchev toured the country. He used face-to-face meetings with local party officials to win additional support.

Khrushchev also made promises. He pledged to raise food output. However, unlike Malenkov, Khrushchev promised to do it cheaply and without taking resources from heavy industry or the military. His idea was to plow up millions of acres in Central Asia and western Siberia that had never been farmed before, the so-called Virgin Lands program. This area, larger than the entire cropland of Canada, had never been cultivated because of inadequate rainfall. This did not stop Khrushchev. Whatever the environmental limits, to him the resources of this under-developed area were "inexhaustible." His plan was to mobilize tens of thousands of people, especially the youth, and send them to these new farming regions in the east.

This was done, beginning in 1954, with some going voluntarily and some by force. It was a huge undertaking. The region had no roads, no storage facilities, not even buildings to house the farmer/pioneers Khrushchev was sending there. None of this bothered Khrushchev at all, especially after he toured the region in the spring of 1954.

> *The trip gave me my first chance to see what that part of our country was like. I was struck by the wide-open spaces. Sometimes I would have to drive for hours before I would come to a settlement of tents near a plowed field. Sometimes I'd be driving along and see a tractor like a tiny speck on the horizon. The people . . . used to say a tractor driver could have breakfast at one end of a field, lunch at the other end, and dinner back where he'd started out in the morning.* 3

The local population did not share Khrushchev's enthusiasm for his pet project. In Kazakhstan, the huge but lightly populated Soviet republic that occupies most of Central Asia, ethnic Kazakhs feared they would be swamped in a sea of alien Russians. Because of their insufficient enthusiasm for his scheme, Khrushchev replaced both the first and second secretaries of the local Communist party. The man Khrushchev chose as the new local second secretary was a tough official who had caught his eye in the Ukraine—Leonid Brezhnev. Brezhnev, who one day would take Khrushchev's job from him, soon was promoted to be Kazakhstan's first secretary. He became Khrushchev's key man on the spot during the crucial first years of the Virgin Lands experiment.

In 1954, despite hardship and mistakes, the virgin lands yielded a good crop. This came at an excellent time for Khrushchev, who needed all of the ammunition he could get in his struggle against Malenkov.

By February 1955 Malenkov was outmaneuvered. He resigned as prime minister. His reasons were curious, at least to anyone who knew the Soviet Union. Malenkov, who had been so close to Stalin and managed the economic recovery after World War II, cited his "inexperience" in industrial matters. He also took the blame for agricultural difficulties. Nobody mentioned that Khrushchev, not Malenkov, was in charge of agriculture since 1953.

After February 1955 Khrushchev was the most powerful politician in the Soviet Union, but his position was not secure. Malenkov's place as prime minister was taken by Nikolai Bulganin, who had been a close associate of Khrushchev's ever since the two worked together in Moscow in the 1930s. But Malenkov was not finished politically. Far from it. He retained his influential position on the party Presidium. He also had many well-placed allies. Khrushchev had managed to squeeze into the driver's seat, but he was surrounded on all sides by powerful back-seat drivers. He could maintain his position only if he kept their support. If he misjudged the road and hit a rut, somebody else would be ready to grab the wheel. Khrushchev knew this, and what he did over the next two years reflected his uneasy situation.

It is a measure of the enormous pressure for reform and the degree of consensus among the leadership that so much changed even as this struggle for power was played out. In 1953 the government admitted that the "Doctors' Plot" was a hoax. The surviving doctors were then released. That same year there was also welcome economic news for the long-suffering Soviet consumers. Food prices were cut by an average of 10 percent. Collective farm peasants benefited from lower taxes, higher prices for their products, and lower quotas on goods they had to deliver to the state. These reforms reinforced each other, benefiting both producers and consumers. The peasants' low standard of living rose a little. At the same time, they were given incentives to produce more. This they did, increasing the amount of available food and thereby improving the diet for the population as a whole.

Meanwhile, four thousand political prisoners were released from the Gulag. Although millions were left behind, the release of this small group, whose members were usually well connected, increased the pressure to consider the others. For example, among those released in the first wave were Molotov's wife and Khrushchev's daughter-in-law. By 1955 the number released reached twelve thousand. Among them were many people Khrushchev had worked with under Stalin.

This post-Stalin "thaw," as it is usually called, after a 1954 Soviet novel of that name, also extended to cultural affairs. A number of writers began to touch on subjects forbidden during Stalin's lifetime. These included corruption in the party and the damage Stalin's policies had done to the arts. Some forbidden books were returned to the shelves. These changes, however, were very limited, and in 1955 there was a partial reversal of even these limited reforms.

Another area of change was foreign affairs. By 1953 both the Soviet Union and the United States were busy building nuclear weapons and making those weapons increasingly destructive. Given its insecurity at home, the new Soviet leadership moved to lessen tensions with the West. In 1953, an armistice ended the fighting in Korea. The next year an international conference ended the war between French colonial forces and Communist guerrillas in Vietnam. In May 1955 the Soviet Union withdrew its troops from its World War II zone of occupation in Austria and permitted that country to be reunited as a neutral state.

In July, Khrushchev and Bulganin went to Geneva for their first summit meeting with leaders of the United States, Britain, and France. Although Bulganin, as prime minister, technically headed the delegation, there was no doubt that it was really Khrushchev who was in charge. It was his first trip to a Western nation. Khrushchev was very aware that he, a peasant and worker with a limited education, would have to deal with the polished and privileged leaders of the Western great powers. His reaction to several insignificant events during the conference is revealing. Khrushchev was upset when he noticed that the Western leaders arrived in four-engined planes, while the Soviets had only a two-engined plane. When he met Nelson Rockefeller, the man with the famous name that stands for capitalist wealth, he could not resist poking him in the ribs and saying, "So this is Mr. Rockefeller himself." Still, Khrushchev held his own at Geneva, not only with the American president Dwight D. Eisenhower ("He was a good man, but he wasn't very tough.") but also with his hard-line secretary of state, John Foster Dulles.[4]

While nothing concrete came out of the Geneva meeting, Khrushchev found it to be an important confidence builder:

*We returned to Moscow from Geneva knowing that we hadn't achieved any concrete results. But we were encouraged, realizing that our enemies probably feared us as much as we feared them. . . . The Geneva meeting was an important breakthrough for us on the diplomatic front. We had established ourselves as able to hold our own in the international arena.[5]*

Khrushchev made two other important trips in 1955. The first, during May and June, was to Yugoslavia. Yugoslavia was a Communist state whose leader, Marshal Tito, had broken away from the Communist bloc in 1948 after a dispute with Stalin. Although some of the Soviet leadership, especially Foreign Minister Molotov, opposed the move, Khrushchev led a delegation to try to patch up the feud.

The visit got off on the wrong foot. When the Soviet

delegation arrived at the Yugoslav airport, Khrushchev gave a speech in which he blamed Beria for all of the trouble. It was an explanation that was absurd to anyone who knew the history of the dispute. Tito made no secret of his anger. He did not even bother to have Khrushchev's speech translated for the airport audience. Later in the visit Khrushchev did not do his reputation as a diplomat any good when he became drunk and passed out at an official reception. This time Tito was more helpful: he assisted in carrying Khrushchev from the reception through the crowd of assembled guests.

Khrushchev learned from his mistakes in Yugoslavia. Well before the end of his visit he clearly was becoming more skilled at handling both diplomacy and public appearances. Overall, the trip was a partial success. Yugoslavia and the Soviet Union resumed state-to-state relations. But Tito refused to reestablish the type of party-to-party relations the Soviet Communist Party enjoyed with the Communist parties of its Eastern European satellites. Still, Khrushchev did well enough so that when he needed Tito's help the following year he received it.

Khrushchev and Bulganin were more successful in improving relations with the non-Communist nations of Asia and Africa. They made a very well received trip to India, Burma, and Afghanistan. Their best results were in India, the world's most populous non-Communist nation, where they established a solid relationship that endures to this day.

Another important friendship was established with Egypt, the most populous nation in the Arab world. The Soviets began courting the Egyptians in 1955. Their real break came in 1956. In the fall of that year, in retaliation for years of deadly Egyptian-sponsored raids against its territory and people, Israel sent its army into Egypt. The Israelis were joined by the British and French. These two American allies were trying to occupy the Suez Canal, which the British had controlled until the Egyptians seized it in 1956. The Soviet Union responded by making loud threats against all three attackers. Although in fact it was

American pressure that made the Israelis, French, and British withdraw from Egypt, the strong Soviet support for Egypt won it many friends in that country and in the rest of the Arab world. Two years later the Soviets strengthened their position in Egypt when Khrushchev agreed to help build the gigantic Aswan Dam on the Nile River.

Trips abroad, however successful, still left Khrushchev's problems at home unresolved. His basic difficulty was that, relative to the enormous problems the country faced, the reforms introduced since 1953 were very few. At the same time, the changes that were introduced, especially the release of twelve thousand prisoners from the Gulag, raised many questions and increased pressure for still more change.

This pressure built as 1956 dawned and the Twentieth Party Congress, the first since Stalin's death, approached. But to introduce greater change meant questioning what had been done under Stalin. This was dangerous, since all of the new Soviet leaders had been deeply involved in carrying out Stalin's brutal policies. Much of the leadership, including Malenkov, Molotov, and Kaganovich, therefore did not want an examination of Stalin or what had been done while he ruled. Their attitude was perhaps best summed up by Presidium member Kliment Voroshilov, Khrushchev's old commander in the Civil War. When he heard of Khrushchev's intention to publicly expose some of Stalin's crimes, he cried out, "But what will happen to us?"[6]

Khrushchev's readiness to face the question of Stalin's crimes, which his colleagues did not share, involved a combination of factors. While he was every bit as brutal and guilty as most of them, he was also different. He alone had always made a point of getting out among the people, whether he worked in Yuzovka, Kiev, or Moscow. He had also been a direct witness to some of the consequences of Stalin's methods during World War II. Seeing the mass desertions to the Germans seems to have convinced him that the Soviet government would have to treat its people differently if it was going to survive. And Khrushchev was not a man to wait when he believed there was an urgent job to be done.

Beyond that, Khrushchev was convinced that the great prosperity communism supposedly promised could be achieved only if the Soviet people were willing to work enthusiastically toward that end. Yet he knew that millions of Soviet workers, from collective farmers to industrial workers, did only what they absolutely had to. Why should they work hard when they were rewarded so badly? To get the people involved, things would have to be done differently than under Stalin. But to do that, Stalin would have to be criticized, since it was his name that gave the old policies their authority.

Finally, Khrushchev probably moved because to do so was smart, although certainly dangerous, politics. Stalin's reputation had been tarnished slightly since 1953. His name was mentioned far less frequently than while he lived, and Lenin's accomplishments were stressed at Stalin's expense. Possibly Khrushchev felt that he had to grab the high ground on the issue before someone else did. Also, if he took the initiative, he could control what was said. This included shifting more of the blame to Malenkov, Molotov, and the others and deflecting it from himself, thereby consolidating his own power while undermining that of his rivals.

When Khrushchev chose to act, he did so with typical boldness. The stage for his great drama was the Twentieth Party Congress. It was set for him in several ways. First, major changes in policy had already been announced at the congress. The new Sixth Five-Year Plan included more investment in agriculture and consumer goods. In place of the old Leninist doctrine of the inevitability of war between capitalism and communism, a new resolution proclaimed the doctrine of "peaceful coexistence" between the rival systems. There was even some criticism of Stalin in a speech by Anastas Mikoyan, a veteran party leader.

*During a closed-door session of the Twentieth Party Congress
of the Communist Party, Khrushchev delivered
a speech that stunned both his countrymen and the West.*

Most important, at a heated meeting of the Presidium that took place during the congress, Khrushchev won agreement to report on a commission that had been investigating Stalin's crimes. He got his way over the strong objection of Molotov, Kaganovich, and the fearful Voroshilov. Khrushchev's main compromise was to agree to deliver his speech at a closed session of the congress. Only the delegates would be present; no outside guests or members of the press were permitted to attend. This concession was more than offset by the fact that the other

Presidium members did not see the text of Khrushchev's speech before he delivered it.

Khrushchev's speech was a political show-stealer, a virtuoso performance. It was a lightning bolt that illuminated at least part of a Soviet historical sky blackened for a generation by lies. On the night of February 24–25, just when most of the delegates thought their work was done, Khrushchev called them together in a closed session for what is called his "Secret Speech." He spoke for four-and-one-half hours. Often he ad-libbed, departed from his text, or spoke from personal experience. The delegates sat in shocked silence. As Khrushchev recalls: "It was so quiet in the huge hall you could hear a fly buzzing."[7]

As Khrushchev spoke, the Communist closet burst open and the skeletons came tumbling out. He accused Stalin of being a brutal dictator. Stalin had murdered thousands of loyal Communists during the Great Purge. During World War II he had made blunders that cost enormous losses of life. His blood-letting had damaged many areas of Soviet life, from the economy to the government to the nation's ability to defend itself against the Germans. Adding insult to injury, Stalin had glorified himself beyond reason and taken credit for what others had done. This last offense Khrushchev called Stalin's "cult of personality." He revealed Lenin's distrust of Stalin and insisted that Stalin had betrayed Leninist ideals:

> Lenin used severe methods only in the most necessary cases. . . . Stalin, on the other hand, used extreme methods and mass repressions at a time when the revolution was already victorious. . . . it is clear that here Stalin showed in a whole series of cases his intolerance, his brutality, and his abuse of power. Instead of proving his political correctness and mobilizing the masses, he often chose the path of repression and physical annihilation, not only against actual enemies, but also against individuals

*who had not committed any crimes against the Party and the Soviet government.* [8]

Although this was devastating information, Khrushchev also left out a lot. He ignored the millions of peasants killed during collectivization. He never spoke of the cruel hardships of the industrialization drive. He did not mention the millions of nonparty victims of the purges. Nor did Stalin's political opponents during the 1920s, the men who had made the revolution with Lenin, receive their due. The party itself, as distinct from Stalin, was above criticism, as was everything Stalin did before 1934.

The "Secret Speech" did not remain a secret for long. In the West, the U.S. Department of State got hold of a copy and published it a few months later. In the Soviet Union rumors quickly spread. Although the speech was not published, it was read at thousands of party regional and district meetings to stunned members.

Khrushchev's speech proved to be a two-edged sword and a very sharp one. It cut very deeply into Malenkov, Molotov, and Kaganovich, the men closest to Stalin when his crimes were committed. Khrushchev therefore weakened his opponents. Yet the speech cut dangerously close to the entire Soviet system. After all, what kind of system and what kind of men would permit Stalin to commit so many terrible crimes for so long? In fact, Khrushchev was asked exactly this question during a later speech. He was handed a note from the audience demanding to know how he and the others in power could have permitted these crimes. When Khrushchev in turn demanded to know who had written the note, nobody stood up. Khrushchev then admitted he understood why the note's author lacked the courage to stand up, adding "we were afraid to stand up against Stalin."

This answer was not enough. Soon Khrushchev himself was in deep trouble. In Georgia, Stalin's homeland, riots against

Khrushchev's speech required troops to restore order. The pressure for more information and reforms built. It became more intense during 1956 and 1957 when over 8 *million* people were released from the Gulag and returned to their homes. There were calls to punish the guilty. This, of course, would have been suicidal, since so many in the party were involved in Stalin's crimes. A few officials were punished lightly but little more. This led to anger and cynicism, summed up nicely by an unknown poet:

> *Without mourning flags on the state's towers,*
> *Without funeral speeches or candles,*
> *Russia forgave the innocent who had been punished,*
> *And also forgave her executioners.* 9

Worse news soon came from Eastern Europe, where after World War II Stalin had imposed Communist governments on the local people. These governments were brutal and unpopular. Nationalism and dislike for the Russians ran high in many of the countries. After Khrushchev's speech they ran out of control in two: Poland and Hungary. In Poland, bloody riots broke out in June 1956. By October the pressures on the old-line Stalinist rulers were enough to force major changes. Wladyslaw Gomulka, an independent-minded Communist recently released from prison, crowned his comeback by being elected party head. Although he had no intention of leaving the Communist bloc, Gomulka wanted a small measure of independence for Poland. He stood up to the Soviets and to the threat of military force when Khrushchev led an angry delegation to Poland. When Khrushchev became convinced that Poland would fight if Soviet troops moved against the new Polish leadership, he backed down. Gomulka was allowed to introduce reforms in Poland, including abolishing the hated collective farms.

If the pot boiled over in Poland, it exploded in Hungary. Huge demonstrations began there late in October 1956. Clashes erupted between Soviet troops and demonstrators, who began to arm themselves. Then part of the Hungarian army joined the demonstrators in fighting the hated foreign occupiers. Within days these reform pressures produced results. A worried party leadership elected Imre Nagy, a popular party figure with a reputation for independence, as the country's prime minister. Nagy requested that Soviet troops, in Hungary since the World War II, leave the country. Then came the bombshell. Nagy announced that Hungary would no longer be a one-party Communist dictatorship. It was leaving the Warsaw Pact, the Soviet-dominated military alliance, and becoming a neutral nation like Austria.

This Khrushchev and his colleagues would not tolerate. For those who might have forgotten, Khrushchev now demonstrated once again that he could be as tough and treacherous as the circumstances dictated. The Presidium voted unanimously to use military force to bring Hungary back into the fold. But sending the Red Army against a fellow Communist regime was unprecedented. The men in the Kremlin therefore sought the approval of China and Yugoslavia, the two Communist states that were in fact independent of Moscow. A high-level Chinese delegation went to Moscow and after some hesitation agreed to a Soviet invasion of Hungary. Khrushchev and Malenkov then flew to Yugoslavia to get Tito's approval. That they flew in terrible weather to visit Tito on an island off the Yugoslav coast indicates just how urgent the problem was. Aside from the weather, Khrushchev undoubtedly was worrying about Tito's reaction and about his own political future if the crisis ended badly. Malenkov, as Khrushchev recalls, had additional concerns:

> *The weather couldn't have been worse. We had to fly through the mountains in a fierce thunderstorm. Lightning was flashing all around us. I didn't sleep a wink. I had flown a great deal, especially during the war, but I'd never flown in conditions this bad. . . . But . . . we made it. . . . Malenkov was pale as a corpse. He gets carsick on a*

*good road. We had just landed after the roughest flight imaginable and now we were heading out into choppy seas in a small launch. Malenkov lay down in the boat and shut his eyes. I was worried what kind of shape he'd be in when we docked, but we didn't have any choice. As the old Russian saying goes, we couldn't sit on the beach and wait for good weather.* [10]

Khrushchev and Malenkov were relieved to learn that Tito supported the invasion. Soviet troops began to move on No-vember 1. In response to Hungarian protests, the Soviets as-sured Nagy that no invasion was planned. This act of treachery was skillfully carried out by the Soviet ambassador to Hungary, Yuri Andropov, later to become the leader of the Soviet Union.

In fact, the invasion had begun. Soviet troops backed by three thousand tanks swept into Hungary. The Hungarians resisted. Thousands were killed in bitter but hopeless fighting. Over two hundred thousand refugees fled to the West. Nagy and several other Hungarian leaders fled to the Yugoslav embassy. After leaving the embassy with a promise of safe-conduct, they were seized and taken to Moscow. They were executed in 1958.

The uprisings in Poland and Hungary very nearly included Khrushchev among their victims. They strengthened the argu-ments and influence of Malenkov, Molotov, and their allies. These men had opposed Khrushchev's "destalinization," warn-ing that it threatened unrest in the entire Soviet system. Khru-shchev knew he was in trouble. He backtracked, even finding the words to praise Stalin. He attacked writers who had crit-icized Stalin. His opponents became bolder. During late 1956 and early 1957 a reorganization in the government weakened him and strengthened his opponents.

Shortly thereafter Khrushchev counterattacked. It was a typically bold step. He called for a total reorganization of the governmental bodies that planned and ran the economy. Insist-ing that the central ministries responsible for the economy seldom knew what was going on at the local level, Khrushchev abolished 140 of them. He then divided the country into 105 regional economic councils called *sovnarkhozy*. Each of these new units was responsible for the entire economy within its local geographic area. All of this naturally required moving thousands of administrators around. Khrushchev just as naturally used this to promote his supporters and demote his opponents. To build support for this controversial program, Khrushchev promised that the Soviet Union would be able to match the United States in milk, butter, and meat production in three to four years.

The *sovnarkhozy* scheme and Khrushchev's impossible promises became the last straw. Malenkov, Molotov, and the other old-line Stalinists, joined by Khrushchev's old colleague, Prime Minister Bulganin, organized their forces on the Presidium. When the Presidium met on June 19, 1957, they removed Khrushchev from office by a vote of seven to four.

The battle should have been over right there, but it was not. As they had done several years earlier, Khrushchev's opponents underestimated him. He refused to resign. Bulganin protested: "But we are seven and you are four," only to have Khrushchev respond, "Certainly, in arithmetic two and two make four. But politics is not arithmetic. It is something different."[11]

The reason the vote in the Presidium did not add up was that Khrushchev insisted that, according to party rules, the Presidium's decision had to be confirmed by the Central Committee. It proved impossible for the Presidium majority to deny Khrushchev's demand. News of the stormy meeting already had gotten out, and many of the Central Committee members, including Khrushchev supporters, were already in Moscow. Now Khrushchev was helped by one of his ties to the military. Marshal Zhukov, of World War II fame, had become defense minister; he provided military planes that brought Khrushchev's supporters to Moscow from all over the country for the decisive Central Committee meeting.

Khrushchev triumphed in the Central Committee showdown. Malenkov, Molotov, and Kaganovich—denounced as the "anti-party group"—were dismissed from the Presidium and their government posts. Still, unlike what would have happened to them in Stalin's day, they survived physically. Malenkov and Molotov were given minor jobs. So was Kaganovich, the old hatchet man, who tearfully phoned Khrushchev begging for mercy. Bulganin was allowed to stay in his prime minister's job for a short while. Zhukov, Khrushchev's savior, was promoted to the Presidium. Khrushchev packed the Presidium with his supporters. Among them was Yekaterina Furtseva, the only woman to sit on the Politburo (1957–1961) from the founding of the Soviet state until Mikhail Gorbachev appointed a woman as a *candidate,* or nonvoting, member in 1988. (Furtseva was a *full,* voting member.)

But the most important thing by far was what was not done. Two years earlier, in 1955, political scores had been settled without bloodshed for the first time since the 1920s. Khrushchev now decisively confirmed that rejection of Stalinist methods. Soviet politics remained rough, but never again would it demand the lives of the losers. Just as Khrushchev had defeated his opponents, so had the new politics defeated the old. Years later, when he finally was voted out of office, Khrushchev would say that making that vote possible was his most important achievement. There is little doubt that he was right.

Khrushchev soon followed up his June victory. In October 1957 he eliminated a potential rival by removing Zhukov from his posts. That same month came one of the greatest triumphs of Khrushchev's term in office and one of the proudest moments in Soviet history. The Soviets launched *Sputnik,* the world's first artificial satellite. In March 1958 Bulganin was removed as prime minister. Khrushchev took that job himself. Like Stalin before him, Khrushchev now held the top posts in both the party (First Secretary) and the state (Prime Minister). Although he lacked Stalin's power, he was by far the most powerful man in the Soviet Union. What remained was to use that power to realize his dreams for his country.

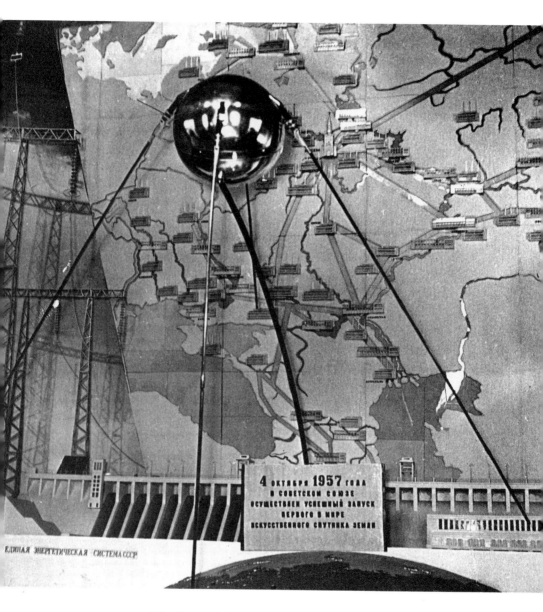

The Soviets' "moment of glory" came in
October 1957, when they launched Sputnik I,
the world's first satellite, into space.

# SIX
## KHRUSHCHEV IN COMMAND: 1958-1961

Although Khrushchev's term at the top of the Soviet political mountain spans the years 1953 to 1964, his peak years of success and power were from 1958 to 1961. Before 1958 Khrushchev first had to struggle for power and then solidify his position. After 1961 he suffered a series of setbacks that reduced his stature and eventually resulted in his fall. Between those rough upward and downward slopes lay the real high ground of Khrushchev's political career.

This ground was typical of the man and the times in which he lived. It was not a plateau, smooth and flat, where Khrushchev could maneuver with relative ease without running into unexpected obstacles or hidden traps. Rather it was a jagged, pockmarked political landscape, with summits that Khrushchev scaled daringly and valleys into which he stumbled clumsily, all with dizzying speed and without a moment's pause to rest.

As with any other national leader, much of what Khrushchev did even at the peak of his power was determined by events and forces beyond his control. It is vital to understand this. Many of Khrushchev's policies reflected the outlook of the Soviet leadership as a whole. When they did not, Khrushchev often got his way despite considerable opposition. If these controversial policies ran into trouble, Khrushchev's opponents sometimes became strong enough to force him to reverse himself. Often this produced confusion and even more trouble. Also, both at home and abroad the Soviet Union faced problems that no single leader had caused or could solve. How Khrushchev responded to them frequently depended on what others did or how the situations developed independent of anyone's ability to control them.

At the same time, Khrushchev did hold great power in his hands. He also had a very strong personality and his own distinct way of reacting to challenges. These personal factors are very important in explaining why Khrushchev followed certain policies. They also help to explain why his policies succeeded or failed.

One of the keys to understanding Khrushchev's methods is that he was an idealist in the fullest sense of the word. Khrushchev not only believed in the ideal of communism as outlined by Karl Marx, he believed that it could be realized. He further believed it could be realized in the Soviet Union and in a relatively short time. In 1959, when he told the Twenty-first Party Congress that his new program, developed over the past two years, would lead to the "full scale construction of communism," he sincerely believed it could happen. Leading Soviet officials might be cynical about these prospects. Some party members might joke or—as they did at one meeting in Moscow—even laugh openly at the suggestion that a date could be fixed for the full realization of communism. Not Khrushchev. He was perfectly serious when he told the Twenty-second Party Congress in 1961 that the "present generation" of Soviet citizens would live under communism.

Nor was Khrushchev's vision of a Communist utopia limited to the Soviet Union. Thus, he was not threatening but simply predicting, and perhaps bragging, when he told Americans that their children would live under communism.

Like many idealists, Khrushchev was also impatient.

Whether he expected to be around when the "present genera-tion" achieved communism is hard to tell. He was, after all, well past sixty when he was making his predictions. But he certainly intended to see the outline of communism, if not the whole picture, before he left the scene. As early as 1957 he had begun predicting that each Soviet citizen would have more meat, milk, and butter than each American within a few years. American dairy production, he said, was to be passed by 1961. In 1959 Khrushchev had the Five-Year Plan for 1956–60 scrapped. His new Seven-Year Plan called for reaching overall U.S. levels in output per person and consumer welfare by 1970. None of these boasts or plans panned out. If they had, Khrushchev would have seen some of his dream come true. Although he never predicted how long he would live, he survived until 1971.

All of this idealism and haste to do good had its negative side. Because he had such high goals and so little time to realize them, Khrushchev was willing to try high-risk, unproven methods to save time. One of these was his Virgin Lands campaign. Another was his plan to grow corn in large parts of the Soviet Union. He listened to what in reality were crackpot schemes to improve agriculture because they promised quick results at minimum costs. This accounts for the influence of a pseudo-scientist named Trofim Lysenko, whose ideas damaged both Soviet agriculture and Soviet science. The *sovnarkhozy* plan of 1957 to reorganize virtually the entire Soviet economy was another quick-fix scheme, as was a plan announced in 1962 to split the Communist party in half, one part to deal with industry and the other with agriculture. The best known and most dangerous of Khrushchev's quick-fix schemes was his at-tempt in 1962 to protect the Communist regime of Fidel Castro and at the same time overcome American nuclear missile supe-riority by installing Soviet missiles in Cuba. It led as will be seen (see p. 136) to the Cuban Missile Crisis, the very brink of war, and an embarrassing and damaging Khrushchev retreat.

At times Khrushchev's daring and risk-taking paid off. His

[102]

1956 speech against Stalin is a classic example of this. The Virgin Lands produced some good crops, at least for a while. But many of his schemes did not work. When they failed, Khrushchev was likely to try new quick-fixes to undo the damage of the old ones. Generally, these produced more disappointment. Some basically sound policies that might have worked had they been introduced slowly and with careful planning were ruined or damaged because Khrushchev insisted that everything be done so quickly. Also, sometimes Khrushchev suddenly reversed himself. This not only led to confusion but eventually turned many of his supporters against him.

While Khrushchev often acted too quickly, he cannot be accused of failing to get firsthand information on the problems he faced. Rarely, in fact, has any national leader made such an effort to see things for himself. The open, hands-on style of Yuzovka and the Ukraine remained Khrushchev's style after he reached the Kremlin.

Shortly after Stalin's death Khrushchev opened the Kremlin to the public for the first time since 1930. But he was never satisfied to let the people come to him. He went to them. Beginning in 1953 Khrushchev toured the Soviet Union constantly. He visited the farms and factories to observe conditions, rally support for his programs, and give advice. Several times he toured the Virgin Lands. One of his most extensive tours, in 1961, took him to the Ukraine, the Caucasus, the Ural Mountains region, Siberia, and Central Asia. Altogether, with time out for one stopover in Moscow, Khrushchev was on the road for more than two months. As if this were not enough, at the end of the year he took another tour of Soviet agricultural regions that ranged from the western part of the country far east into Siberia.

Khrushchev's determination to learn things for himself at first hand was not limited to the Soviet Union or his fellow Soviet citizens. He also made time to meet foreigners in Moscow, whether they happened to be media correspondents, private citizens, or diplomats. He knew many of the foreign correspondents and could address them by name at news conferences. Foreign businessmen or artists found him available for meetings. Diplomats often found that their meetings with him went beyond the usual formalities. A British ambassador recalled one such incident:

> On another occasion I arrived at his office with a message . . . which I said I would just leave with him and return later for his reply. He insisted, however, that I must stay, because no one ever saw him for less than an hour. If I left him at once his staff would think our countries were going to war. He would not, however, open the envelope until after I had left and meanwhile we might have a general conversation, for example on books we had each been reading. It emerged he was in the middle of War and Peace, which he tried to reread every year and from which he quoted long passages, as I afterwards checked, with great accuracy. When it was my turn and I mentioned Turgenev's Sportsmen's Sketches, he at once showed his familiarity with it. I have rarely passed a more surprising and agreeable hour. [1]

Khrushchev did not limit himself to conversations with diplomats in his effort to learn about the world outside the Soviet Union's borders. It was a world that, prior to 1953, he knew almost nothing about. On one level he had begun to make peace with that vast unknown. Nuclear weapons, he insisted, meant that capitalist and Communist countries, whatever their differences, had to avoid war. They would compete but within the framework of "peaceful coexistence," the doctrine announced at the Twentieth Party Congress in 1956.

Yet Khrushchev continued to view the West through a crude Marxist prism that divided capitalist societies into workers and capitalists. Even in his later years, when he had seen a lot of the West, this stereotype remained in Khrushchev's mind. He seems to have been fascinated by millionaires and how they lived. This helps to account for his reaction to Nelson Rockefeller in Geneva in 1955, as well as to other wealthy people he met in the United States and other Western countries. His memoirs are laced with comments like "A capitalist is a capitalist" and "Well, I've got to remember these men are capitalists," even though it is clear that Khrushchev learned to distinguish between "capitalists" with whom he could do business and those with whom he could not.[2] Khrushchev even began to fancy himself a bit of an expert on the subject of wealthy life-styles. In his memoirs he recalls his visit to President Eisenhower's farm, noting confidently that while it was the home of a wealthy man, it was not up to the standard of a millionaire.

Khrushchev also took to the West a combination of nationalist pride mixed with a nagging inferiority complex. In this he was not special. It is a characteristic Westerners have observed in Russians for centuries. Khrushchev knew that the Soviet Union lagged behind the West in most technological fields. He therefore wanted to see as many Western factories and farms as possible so that he could help his country improve its methods. He was always interested in how factories operated, how farmers grew their crops, and how the people lived. In his search for useful ideas that could benefit the Soviet Union, no detail, it seems, was too small. For example, while in France the First Secretary of the Communist Party of the Union of Soviet Socialist Republics took time to consider the local pear trees:

*I was also interested to note how the French plant fruit trees, especially pears, in trellised orchards. As a result the branches of the trees are outstretched in a way that makes it easier to pick the fruit. The pickers can select only the ripe fruit, rather than having to shake the fruit out of the tree. You can also plant more trees in a given area [and] you . . . come out ahead economically.*[3]

In the meantime he took great pride when the Soviet Union demonstrated that it too could be a world leader, as it did after 1957 in the early years of space exploration. Khrushchev was delighted when he arrived in the United States in 1959 in the brand-new Soviet jetliner, the Tu-114, and found it was so tall that the Americans did not have a portable staircase high enough to reach the passenger exit:

> *It was an embarrassment for the Americans. They hadn't known our plane was such a giant. We could see the wonder in their eyes as they looked at it. They'd never seen anything like it, and they certainly didn't have anything like it themselves, nor would they for a long time.*4

Khrushchev's remarks in this case actually tell far more about him—particularly his insecurity regarding the United States and his tendency to brag to hide his fears—than about the Americans he is trying to describe. While the situation may have been a bit awkward, there was nothing about Khrushchev's aircraft to cause the Americans to wonder or be amazed. The Tu-114 was nothing more than the civilian version of the Soviet Tu-95 Bear bomber, a plane in operation since the mid-1950s. The Tu-95 Bear certainly was an impressive aircraft. But it was both smaller and slower than the mighty American B-52, the world's most powerful bomber at the time, which had been part of the U.S. arsenal since the *early* 1950s.

While his most important trip abroad was his 1959 visit to the United States, Khrushchev's travels stretched far afield, from France in Western Europe to China in East Asia. When he was in the West, Khrushchev was always trying to get out and meet people. In this he was far more like traditional Western politicians than a Soviet one. His memoirs record satisfaction when he succeeded and frustration when he failed. He was, in fact, at his best when he could mix with working people, regardless of the country involved. He had many enjoyable meetings with foreign working people, but one, on a rural road in France, stands out. In this case the Russian ex-mineworker got a chance not only to talk to French workers but to work beside them:

> So Rodion Yakovlevich [Malinovsky, the Soviet defense minister] and I got in our car and drove out of Paris along one of those beautiful French country roads lined with full, shady linden trees. It was a warm sunny day, but . . . at one point the road was blocked by a fallen linden tree. Along came a road repair crew with axes and saws to clear the tree off the road. I took an ax from one of the workers and began to chop away furiously, so that the chips were flying. The French people gathered around pointing and laughing: here was the Russian Prime Minister wielding an ax like a woodcutter! . . . The photographers and movie cameramen were recording this whole scene on film. I knew it wouldn't do our delegation's image any harm for people to see that our government is made up of workers and that the head of our government, despite his age, could still do strenuous work with his hands. When we finished cutting the tree in half, we dragged the pieces to the side of the road, got back in our car and drove on.[5]

Khrushchev's encounters with the general population in the West seem to have met with the approval of other Communist party leaders. They were less pleased with his contacts with ordinary people back in the Soviet Union. This was because Khrushchev tried to use the population as a whole to put pressure on party officials who opposed his programs. One technique was to go touring and make promises, often very unrealistic ones, about the prosperity his programs would bring. Another was to invite nonparty citizens to attend party meetings, even meetings of the Central Committee. For the millions of citizens who could not attend, Khrushchev ordered that the minutes of these meetings be published. That way the people could see just who was behind their leader and who was making things difficult.

Aside from the fact that dealing directly with ordinary people came naturally to Khrushchev, there was a practical political reason for his use of popular pressure. Like any established group, many party officials did not want to change the policies and methods they knew, those left over from Stalin. Khrushchev was convinced that in order to build communism these methods *had* to be changed. But how was he to move the party? He could not use the secret police to terrorize party officials. Those days were over, in large part due to Khrushchev himself. He could and did replace people. However, this took time, and often even people he appointed were attached to the old ways.

Khrushchev therefore turned to popular pressure. His use of the people to pressure the party was one of the things that made him different from other Soviet leaders. But it also made Khrushchev controversial. Party officials, who were used to giving orders rather than listening to complaints, felt threatened. No doubt this technique contributed to some of his successes. Yet in the long run it made powerful people angry, and this anger would haunt Khrushchev when some of his policies began to falter.

There was one other central aspect of Khrushchev's complex and contradictory political style. While he would appeal for popular support, he was *not* a believer in democracy in any sense of the word. Nikita Khrushchev's power was based completely on the dictatorship of the Communist party. After the harm the party had suffered under Stalin, Khrushchev did a great deal to restore it to the position it had enjoyed prior to the Great Purge. The party had written rules, and Khrushchev insisted that they be followed. Its various bodies met regularly, from the Presidium's weekly sessions to the party congresses every three years.

But there was no room in Khrushchev's political universe to let the *people* decide. He wanted to help the farmers, but he would not let *them* run their farms. He might allow artists and writers more freedom than Stalin had, but if they went too far, he would crack down—hard. He did not execute party opponents. But he fired officials in large numbers and greeted their shortcomings with charges that they had committed "crimes" or "sins."

Once he was firmly in charge, Khrushchev faced many pressing problems. One of the most important was to raise the Soviet standard of living. This was crucial not only to avoid discontent but because of Khrushchev's view about the struggle between communism and capitalism. He believed nuclear war would destroy both the West and the Communist countries and that peaceful coexistence was therefore necessary. This meant the two systems would have to compete in other ways. In Khrushchev's view, the system that could provide the highest standard of living would be the one to triumph. Therefore, the Soviet Union, whose living standards were far lower than in the West, had to raise those standards as quickly as possible.

To do this obviously required improving the economy in general and agriculture in particular. Despite the significant improvements between 1953 and 1957, Soviet farmers still lived badly and did not produce enough food to feed the country properly. Khrushchev's dream was to improve the farmers' life in every respect, and fast. If his policies were followed, he promised, not only would they be producing more, they would soon have the most modern luxuries of life:

> *Sturdy production buildings, well appointed residences, clubs, schools and boarding schools, libraries, communal services establishments, good roads, electricity, radio, television, cinema—such are the realistic features of the Soviet village of the not remote future.* [6]

As usual, Khrushchev suggested a drastic step to begin creating the future Soviet village. At the time of collectivization, alongside the new collective farms, institutions called Machine

Tractor Stations had been set up. In theory, the MTSs existed for efficiency reasons. They would have highly trained staffs to maintain the complex modern agricultural machinery the collectives needed. Each MTS would provide machinery for several collectives so that the expensive machines could be used as widely as possible. In reality, the MTS network was another means of bleeding the collectives. They charged the collectives a high rent for their machines. Yet often the machines were not available when the collectives needed them. Adding injury to injury, the collectives had to pay their rent whether they got their machines in time or not, or even at all.

Abolishing the MTS system was a sound idea. The problem is that it was done too quickly and without allowing the collectives any choices in what they bought. Most of this huge network, with its enormous stock of machinery, was dismantled in three *months*. Collectives were forced to buy the MTS machines. Payment had to be made quickly. No allowance was made for the differences between prosperous and poor collectives in their ability to pay. Used machines were sold at *new* equipment prices, which were set by the state and were very high. Nor was consideration given to how the collectives would maintain this equipment by themselves. These and other problems led to chaos. Collectives were loaded down with additional debt, and valuable machines were ruined because of inadequate maintenance.

Corn was another Khrushchev cure for Soviet agricultural problems. He was convinced that corn was the perfect crop to produce the animal feed necessary for the Soviet Union to increase its cattle herds. This in turn would permit the large increases in milk and meat production he wanted so badly.

Khrushchev was not without experience in corn production. He had grown corn at his country home when he moved to Moscow after World War II, producing stalks that, he proudly reported, reached above a man's head. Next he had corn planted on a collective farm nearby.

*The results were phenomenal. I took members of the Presidium to see how well the experiment turned out. The chairman of the collective farm demonstrated how tall the corn was by riding through the field on horseback—you couldn't even see the top of his head until he came to the road.*[7]

Khrushchev's 1959 visit to America, where he found some truth to the claim in the popular song "Oh What a Beautiful Morning" that the "corn is as high as an elephant's eye and it looks like it's climbing clear up to the sky," reinforced his convictions. Actually, his corn drive began in 1954. Corn acreage was quadrupled over the next two years. This was more than enough. Climate and soil conditions, so favorable to corn in Iowa, were far less suited to corn in most of the USSR. Yet after 1957 Khrushchev used his power to force yet another doubling of corn acreage over the next five years. Even at the beginning the results were very disappointing. In the early 1960s they became disastrous.

Yet another Khrushchev quick fix was to go out into the provinces and stir up enthusiasm. The idea was to get local officials to commit their districts to double or triple their production of one food or another. Presumably, this new spirit would get people to work harder and unlock all sorts of unrealized potential. In one highly publicized case, Khrushchev seemed to have succeeded. Early in 1959 the party first secretary in the Riazan region southeast of Moscow pledged to more than double his area's production of meat that year. Sure enough, by the end of the year the region reported that it had *tripled* its deliveries of meat to the state. The region's first secretary was duly honored with the prestigious Order of Lenin award.

It soon came out just how so much meat had been delivered so quickly. Breeding stock and dairy cattle had been slaughtered, mortgaging both future meat and dairy production for one year's supply of meat. Meat was purchased in neighboring regions at high prices and then brought to Riazan and listed as local production. Other fraudulent methods were used as well. When this deception was exposed in 1960, the local secretary shot himself, leaving Khrushchev to deal with his embarrassment and the anger of his colleagues on the Presidium.

Not all of the agriculture news was bad. Khrushchev continued to reduce the number of collective farms by combining them, further eliminating small and weak farms. The state also continued to increase investment in agriculture, although after 1958 the increases were smaller than during the first five years after Stalin's death. The year 1958 produced a record harvest. This strengthened Khrushchev at the Twenty-first Party Congress, which met in 1959. It also gave him the confidence to make some of his more extravagant promises about future living conditions. But by 1960 his failure to deal with agriculture carefully and systematically caught up with Khrushchev. Problems on the farms continued to dog him for the rest of his years in office.

Matters went slightly more smoothly in industry. Many production goals in heavy industry were met during those years. So were some targets in consumer durables, products such as washing machines and other large appliances. Although quantities of such products, which Americans tend to take for granted, were small relative to the great need, the point was that a serious commitment was being made to give the average Soviet citizen the comforts of modern life.

One consumer durable that Khrushchev did not promote was the automobile. A major concern was that millions of cars in private hands would make it very difficult for the police to keep tabs on the population. There was also an interesting secondary reason. Khrushchev called cars "smelly couches on wheels." He had no desire to see millions of private cars crowding Soviet roads and polluting the air. Looking back through the smog of the late 1980s, he seems to have been a bit of a prophet, at least from an environmental point of view.

Perhaps Khrushchev's greatest achievement for the long-neglected Soviet consumer was housing. This area had been badly neglected under Stalin. In the early and mid-1950s it was common for entire families in urban areas to live in one room in a crumbling building. This was a situation that both concerned and embarrassed Khrushchev:

> I got married in 1914. . . . I found an apartment right away. . . . Years later, after the Revolution, it was painful for me to remember that as a worker under capitalism I'd had much better living conditions than my fellow workers now living under Soviet power. For a long time after the Revolution, we couldn't satisfy even the most elementary needs of our workers. . . . Young couples . . . couldn't even find a place for them in a dormitory. Isn't that awful? . . . How could we expect Soviet man, who'd given his all for the future of socialism and the ultimate victory of Communism, to live in a beehive?[8]

Khrushchev doubled the rate of housing construction between 1955 and 1959. By 1964, the year Khrushchev left office, there was more than twice as much housing as had existed in 1950. What was built was neither the most elegant nor the most durable. Long blocks of dreary apartment houses were thrown up in Soviet cities. Because they were so hastily and sloppily built, many began to deteriorate literally before they were finished. The goal of solving the Soviet housing crisis "within ten or twelve years" was not reached. But whatever the faults in Khrushchev's housing program, it did ease a crisis. This commitment to housing, inadequate and flawed though it was, still was a credit to the Khrushchev regime.

Another area where Khrushchev could claim some success was in improving conditions for scientists. He encouraged the transfer of scientific institutes dealing with specific industries from Moscow and Leningrad to areas where those industries were located. He also had several towns built especially for scientists. Whether this significantly furthered the exchange of ideas among scientists in a country where so much remained secret is debatable. But these towns certainly did improve the living conditions for many scientists, especially younger ones.

The most famous of these communities is the town of Akademgorodok, a suburb of the Siberian city of Novosibirsk. Its scientists and scholars have made a number of significant contributions to Soviet society, most recently as economic advisors to the reforming General Secretary Mikhail Gorbachev. In Khrushchev's time, his sponsorship of science produced a number of spectacular successes in space. These included the launching of the first artificial satellite in 1957, the first landing of a rocket on the moon in 1959, and the first space journey by a human being, Cosmonaut Major Yuri Gagarin, in 1961.

Producing more goods or rocketing men into space was not enough for Khrushchev. Communism, after all, was supposed to mean equality. Yet it was indisputable that some Soviet citizens lived much better than others. Members of the Communist party, especially those nearest the top, lived very much like the wealthy people in capitalist countries. They had the best apartments, enjoyed summer homes, received the best medical care, and could give their children the best available education, to mention just a few of benefits they enjoyed. In terms of the general population, there were great differences in pay beween various professions and between different grades within a given profession. Among the lowest-paid professions were teachers and medical doctors. Also, urban dwellers lived far better than those on the farm, where the most basic necessities, such as indoor plumbing, hardly existed.

To Khrushchev, this situation was intolerable. He introduced a number of measures to lessen inequality. Some were generally accepted. They included reducing taxes on the lowest-paid groups of workers, raising the minimum wage, and abolishing tuition payments for secondary and higher education. Others aroused opposition. One of the most controversial was his education reform. It involved changing both what was being taught and how students were selected for higher education. Its stated purpose was to produce more skilled manpower for factories and farms. At the same time, Khrushchev wanted to change the system by which those with rank and privilege were able to track their children through the best secondary schools into the country's institutions of higher learning. These children looked down on manual labor and factory work, an attitude that Khrushchev found inconsistent with the idea of a Communist society and, as a former herdsman and mine worker, personally insulting. He denounced the "haughty, contemptuous, incorrect attitude" of these young people as "insulting to the toilers of socialist society." He complained, for example, that the number of children of workers and collective farmers in Moscow's institutions of higher education was "practically insignificant."9

Khrushchev's attempt to open the doors to the children of city workers and peasants angered the parents of the elite. And as usual, Khrushchev tried to put his reforms in place too quickly. Although they did have some effect and broke down some barriers, in the end the Soviet educational system remained fundamentally the same.

There were some people who even in Khrushchev's eyes were less equal than others. He responded to increased interest in religion among younger people by increasing antireligious repression. Consistent with a tradition that existed in Russia back in the days of the tsars, Jews were singled out for especially harsh treatment. Khrushchev publicly opposed anti-Semitism and criticized it in others. He attacked Stalin's anti-Semitism, and in his memoirs he denounced the anti-Jewish feelings he found in the Ukraine. But during 1958 and 1959 there was a widespread campaign against Jews. Judaism as a religion was attacked in the press, Jews were arrested and beaten for trying to study their heritage, Israel was viciously denounced, and synagogues were ransacked.

Writers and artists were another group who found that living with Khrushchev could be dangerous. Their experiences with him became an unnerving roller-coaster ride, with steep ups and downs sometimes following each other from month to month. What caused any given reversal is not always certain. As a whole, these shifts involved both Khrushchev's own changes in mood as well as political pressures from within the Presidium and Central Committee. For example, in 1956 a book called *Not by Bread Alone,* by Vladimir Dudintsev, appeared. It exposed corruption in the party. After the troubles in Poland and Hungary that year, the book and its author were denounced.

Then came Boris Pasternak's masterpiece, *Doctor Zhivago.* It focused on the tragic effect the Bolshevik Revolution had on individual people. After being denied permission to publish his book at home, Pasternak sent it to the West, where it was published in 1957. In 1958 he won the Nobel Prize for literature. An avalanche of abuse now fell on Pasternak. He was forced to refuse his Nobel Prize and was hounded until his death a few years later. Yet in 1959 Dudintsev was restored to favor. Then, in 1961, a young poet and admirer of Pasternak, Yevgeny Yevtushenko, was allowed to publish "Babi Yar," a forceful condemnation of Soviet anti-Semitism.

One of the biggest problems Khrushchev had with all of his grand plans—to transform agriculture, build housing, produce consumer goods, promote equality—was that they all cost a great deal of money. This money had to come from somewhere, and one of the places Khrushchev tried to find it was in the military budget. There was general agreement that military spending had to be cut or at least controlled—up to a point. In fact, in 1953, 1955, and 1956, well before Khrushchev solidified his power, defense spending actually decreased slightly.

Khrushchev tried to control the military budget through modernization. His program was to cut the number of troops and to use the money saved on manpower to build modern weapons, especially nuclear weapons. Actually, this program was not unique. The United States under President Eisenhower was doing the same thing, the slogan being that nuclear weapons gave "more bang for the buck" than did conventional arms. Meanwhile, Khrushchev and the Soviet government were trying to get more rumble for the ruble. This was underscored in 1959 with the creation of a new military branch, the Strategic Rocket Forces.

During the late 1950s Khrushchev managed to keep the military budget under control, as did President Eisenhower in the United States. Overall, Soviet military outlays grew slowly. Khrushchev managed this despite constant Cold War tensions, to which he often contributed with his tough language and aggressive foreign policies. Then, in January 1961, Khrushchev announced that Soviet ground forces would be cut by one third. He wanted to use the manpower saved for the civilian economy while continuing to modernize the armed forces as a whole. This program was introduced against the strong opposition of important military circles. With the increase in international tensions that followed, Khrushchev was forced to backtrack. Before the end of the year the manpower cuts were canceled and the military budget increased.

Another military problem was the testing of nuclear weapons. In the 1950s and early 1960s the Soviets and the United States tested many nuclear weapons in the atmosphere. The result was a great deal of radioactive fallout that many people all over the world felt posed a serious long-term health threat. The health issue was one reason Khrushchev was willing to consider some sort of nuclear test ban. Another was his desire to slow the advance of American nuclear technology, which Khrushchev respected and feared. He also wanted to prevent countries like West Germany and the People's Republic of China from becoming nuclear powers.

Therefore, in March 1958, having just finished a series of tests, the Soviet Union announced it was suspending its testing.

Of course, this announcement came just as the United States was about to begin its own series of tests, as the Soviets knew full well. After the Americans had finished their tests, they announced a moratorium of their own, knowing that the Soviets were planning a new test series. After this radioactive round, Khrushchev *again* announced a voluntary testing pause. This one was observed by both sides for almost three years.

In the summer of 1961 the Soviets announced that they would resume testing. Among the people pressuring Khrushchev not to do so was a young nuclear physicist named Andrei Sakharov. Sakharov would later break with the system and become internationally renowned and admired as an advocate of democratic reform in the Soviet Union and winner of the Nobel Peace Prize. In Khrushchev's day he was his country's leading nuclear physicist, the man considered the father of the Soviet hydrogen bomb. Khrushchev and the party leadership rejected Sakharov's request. A series of huge tests followed. The final one, a monstrous explosion equal to 57 megatons (57,000,000 tons of TNT, 2,850 times larger than the bomb that destroyed Hiroshima) set off in the remote Arctic, is the largest explosion ever set off by man. Khrushchev is said to have boasted that it rattled windows in Moscow. Never one for modesty, he then claimed, without offering any proof, that the Soviets had a 100-megaton bomb.

Khrushchev did not intend to leave his impression on the international scene simply by blowing up bombs. He worked hard to present his country in a favorable light to the nations of the world. As usual, he delivered his message in person whenever he could. He was most successful in the newly independent countries of Asia and Africa. They provided the Soviet Union and Khrushchev with a natural audience, as many of these countries resented the Western powers that had so recently been their colonial masters. In early 1960, after his visits to the United States and China and just before he went to France, Khrushchev made a successful Asian tour that took him to India, Indonesia, and Afghanistan.

By far the most important of Khrushchev's foreign journeys was his trip to the United States. During Khrushchev's years at the helm in Moscow, Soviet-American relations ran hot and cold. One of the flash points was Berlin, the capital of prewar Germany. Although the city itself was entirely surrounded by Soviet-dominated East Germany, it was divided into two parts. East Berlin, where Soviet troops were stationed, was the capital of East Germany. West Berlin, still occupied by American, British, and French troops, was part of West Germany, a country now allied with the West. The Soviet goal was to force the Western powers out of West Berlin. Periodically, the Soviets would apply pressure, and there would be a crisis; one occurred in 1958. Naturally, each Berlin crisis worsened Soviet-American relations.

The year 1959 had not been a good year for relations between the two superpowers. During the summer each country had set up an exhibit in the other's capital, a move designed to promote people-to-people contact and improve relations. In July U.S. vice-president Richard M. Nixon visited the American exhibit in Moscow. Khrushchev was there also. The two men engaged in a heated public debate. After the smoke had cleared, Khrushchev made one of his typical unpredictable and dramatic gestures. Nixon gave a speech at the exhibition in which he praised America's freedom of speech and its free press. Khrushchev responded by having Soviet newspapers publish the speech in full.

Given these tensions, Khrushchev was surprised and delighted when President Eisenhower invited him to visit the United States that fall. He was very curious to see America. He admired it as the world's richest and most technologically advanced country. At the same time he feared and resented it as the Soviet Union's major rival. As he later recalled:

*I admit I was curious to have a look at America, although it wouldn't be my first trip abroad. After all, I'd been to England, Switzerland, France, India, Indonesia, Burma, and so on. They were all foreign countries, but they weren't America. America occupied a special place in our thinking and our view of the world. And why shouldn't it? It was our strongest opponent among the capitalist countries, the leader that called the tune of anti-Sovietism for the rest. . . . No wonder we were interested in a firsthand look at our number one capitalist enemy.* [10]

The trip lasted thirteen days, September 15 through 27, and took him from coast to coast. After landing in Washington, Khrushchev saw New York, Los Angeles and Hollywood, San Francisco and San Jose, farm country in Iowa, and industry in Pittsburgh. He then returned to Washington and visited with Eisenhower at the presidential retreat, Camp David, in the Virginia countryside. Khrushchev hoped to establish a good personal relationship with Eisenhower in order to reduce overall tensions and slow the arms race.

The trip certainly had its low points. Khrushchev became visibly angry in public at least twice. The first incident occurred in response to sharp questioning at the National Press Club in Washington, the second after a hostile speech by the mayor of Los Angeles. As conservative in his tastes as he was revolutionary in his politics, Khrushchev was offended by the skimpy clothing and provocative dancing of the actresses on the set of the movie *Can Can*. He felt dancing in which actresses "have to pull up their skirts and show their backsides" catered to "depraved" tastes and was "pornographic." [11] Khrushchev also protested strongly when he was not permitted to visit Disneyland. He was not convinced by the American claim that his security could not be guaranteed at the famous amusement park. It is difficult to imagine any other Soviet leader before or since who would have raised the issue. But it bothered Khrushchev so much that he was still complaining about it when he wrote his memoirs over a decade later.

There were plenty of high points also. Among them was Nina Petrovna Khrushchev, whose calm and dignified presence often contrasted with that of her husband. But Nikita also had his moments. In Los Angeles he spoke of his respect for the American people:

*America is a fine country and its great people are a worthy people. Time was when America was admired by all peoples of the world. It has taught everyone a lesson in industrial development. After the Revolution we set out to learn from the Americans. . . . We learned from you, and you need not be ashamed of your pupils. You should be proud of them, because now we want to catch up with you.* [12]

He thoroughly enjoyed himself in Iowa, especially as he marched with a troop of officials and reporters through a lush cornfield. In a Pittsburgh, Pennsylvania, factory he was at his best, inspecting tools and talking with workers. When one gave him a cigar and a pat on the shoulder, Khrushchev responded by giving the man his watch ("a sturdy steel watch made by our Kuibyshev factory") and a "friendly slap on the shoulder." [13]

The most important part of his trip, however, was not a success. When he and President Eisenhower went to Camp David for their talks, they were unable to make progress in their discussions about the arms race.

Khrushchev's relations with Eisenhower soon deteriorated further. A summit meeting between the two leaders was planned for June 1960 in Paris. Just before the meeting, an American U-2 spy plane was shot down in the Soviet Union. Khrushchev was delighted. The United States had been making such flights for years at heights too great for Soviet planes to reach. They finally succeeded in downing a U-2 with one of their newly developed surface-to-air missiles (SAMs). When Eisenhower refused to apologize for the flights, and in fact took responsibility for them, Khrushchev canceled the summit and angrily denounced Eisenhower.

Things went from bad to worse when Khrushchev decided

to lead the Soviet delegation to the Fifteenth Session of the United Nations General Assembly in New York. He was in New York for several weeks during September and October 1960. In effect he was an uninvited guest of the United States, as he did not need American permission to go to the UN. Khrushchev heightened already existing tensions with several angry speeches. He also angered the Americans when he met with Fidel Castro, who in 1959 led what turned out to be a Communist revolution in Cuba. Khrushchev further shocked everyone when, during a speech he did not like, he removed his shoe and pounded it on his desk in full view of the entire world.

Ironically, Khrushchev and the Soviet Union had as much trouble with Communist China as they did with capitalist America. Both the Soviet Union and the People's Republic of China were Communist states and therefore supposedly allies. The trouble was that Russia and China had border disputes that dated from well before either country's Communist revolution. They involved Russia's seizure of huge amounts of territory from China during tsarist days.

Following the Chinese Revolution in 1949, relations between the two Communist giants had been uneven. Among other things, the Chinese were angry when Khrushchev tried to improve Soviet relations with the United States. The Soviets and Khrushchev feared China's potential power as the most populous nation in the world. This dispute bubbled underground for several years. In 1960 it burst out into the open with angry words from both sides.

Despite his difficulties, Khrushchev maintained his gift for dramatic flourishes. His stage in this case was the Twenty-second Party Congress in October 1961. It was at this congress that the party adopted a new party program, only the third in its

*Khrushchev is flanked by reporters in October 1960, during a United Nations session in New York City.*

history. This was where Khrushchev assured the Soviet people that the current generation would live under communism and that the "foundations of communism" would be built by 1980. By then the production of everything would be doubled, tripled, quadrupled, and so on. Khrushchev also informed his comrades that the Soviet Union was no longer a "dictatorship of the proletariat" but a "state of the whole people." This was an important sign that the country, having moved beyond dictatorship, was indeed getting closer to communism.

Khrushchev had at least three goals at the congress. He wanted to refute the Chinese attacks on the Soviet Union. The Chinese were asserting that they, not the Soviets, were the most revolutionary country in the world and the proper leaders of the world Communist movement. Khrushchev was determined to reassert Soviet leadership. At the same time, he wanted to rekindle mass enthusiasm and idealism at home. His hope was that such spirit would help overcome current economic difficulties. He also wanted to shake up conservative party officials who often opposed his policies and reforms.

These goals demanded, Khrushchev believed, a more complete denunciation of Stalin than had occurred in 1956. This would pull the rug from under the Chinese, who continued to defend Stalin. It would send a message to the Soviet people that Nikita Khrushchev was a dynamic leader who would make up for the hardship they had suffered under Stalin. It would also strike a blow at party conservatives who continued to get in his way.

This time there was no secret speech, Khrushchev spoke in open session before the world. He lashed out at Stalin even harder than he had in 1956. He also went after Malenkov, Molotov, and others by name. A chorus of speeches by other leaders echoed his words. In the end the congress voted to remove Stalin's body from its honored place in Lenin's mausoleum. The job was done the next day. Perhaps Khrushchev and his associates felt like the poet Yevtushenko, who wrote:

*Grimly clenching his embalmed fists,*
*just pretending to be dead, he watched from inside . . .*
*He was scheming. Had merely dozed off.*
*And I, appealing to our government, petition them*
*to double, and treble, the sentries guarding this slab,*
*and stop Stalin from ever rising again and, with Stalin,*
*the past.* [14]

They buried Stalin, not under six feet of earth but under several truck loads of concrete. Statues and monuments of Stalin came tumbling down by the thousands. A wholesale renaming of cities, schools, factories, and other things followed. Not even Stalingrad, the city on the Volga River where the Soviets won their great victory over the Germans in World War II, was spared. It became Volgograd. Yet, for Khrushchev, as 1961 drew to a close, the question remained: Could he bury, with Stalin, the problems the dead tyrant had left behind, as well as the serious new ones that had developed since his death?

# SEVEN
# DECLINE AND FALL

History is full of ironies, situations that are not what they seem. Nikita Khrushchev unknowingly was in one of those situations by 1961. His power and influence seemed to be greater than ever. During the Twenty-second Party Congress and in the months immediately thereafter, he led a devastating assault on Stalin's reputation. Meanwhile, his own stature was growing, nourished by a hearty diet of official propaganda. Early in the year "Khrushchev" became the name of a town in the Ukraine. In June he was suddenly proclaimed one of the leading heroes of World War II, fifteen years after the fighting was over. *Our Nikita Sergeyevich,* a documentary film on his life, was running in the movie theaters. The Soviet media proclaimed him an expert on almost every subject, quoted, as the *New York Times* reported, "on everything from the construction of homes to the eating of horsemeat."[1]

In reality, Khrushchev was a leader in trouble. For years he had been making promises. His ability to persuade people that he could solve problems others could not had helped bring him to power. Now the time had arrived for him to deliver. But the problems he was expected to solve stubbornly refused to go away. The economy failed to meet expectations, especially in agriculture. Foreign policy met with too many embarrassments and defeats. When Khrushchev tried to set things right, with his usual gambles and sudden changes of direction, he antagonized and angered many powerful interest groups in the Soviet Union. Eventually even his long-time supporters began to turn against him, a development Khrushchev may have been aware of but refused to take seriously.

Khrushchev certainly continued to tower above any potential rivals despite his troubles. But he no longer stood securely on a stable pedestal. Nikita Khrushchev was a leader out on a limb. Although he seems not to have noticed, by 1961 that limb had begun to sway as hostile political winds swirled around him ever more strongly. In October 1964 it snapped. His political career came crashing down, leaving him surprised, saddened, and stunned.

One reason Khrushchev was so surprised is that during those years he continued working at his usual furious pace. One of his major concerns remained agriculture. If anything, his concern with agriculture increased, as that vital sector of the economy performed poorly after the good harvest of 1958. The 1961 harvest was yet another disappointment. Khrushchev responded with a new series of programs. The problem was that none of them provided what was needed. Soviet farmers needed more freedom to run their farms and greater incentives to work harder and produce more. Instead, they received more government interference. The agricultural sector as a whole needed more investment for necessities such as rural roads, storage facilities, and fertilizers. But the Soviet government had no money to spare for these necessary but very expensive improvements.

Perhaps the most counterproductive of Khrushchev's policies was his attack on the so-called private sector of Soviet agriculture. Since the 1930s, farmers in the Soviet Union have not had their own farms. Some live on collective farms called kolkhozy, where they work the fields together and receive a share of what is produced based on the work they have done. The rest work on huge state farms called sovkhozy, where they receive a straight salary. However, Soviet farmers have always been allowed to farm tiny garden plots of land on their own time and to do what they want with what they grow. Although these so-called private plots have never accounted for more than 3 or 4 percent of the total Soviet farmland, they have produced as much as 25 percent of the country's food, including at least a third of its milk, fruit, eggs, and vegetables. In short, they have been a vital source of food for the cities and of income for farmers who simply could not survive on what they received from their collective, or state, farms.

Like many party officials, Khrushchev never liked these private plots. He regarded them as remnants of capitalism. He also blamed them for the failure of Soviet farmers to work harder on collective land, reasoning that ignored how little farmers were paid for collective work. In 1958 Khrushchev had tightened restrictions on the private plots. During 1961 and 1962 he did so again. The measures included high taxes and actually forbidding farmers to plant certain crops on their private plots. None of this improved work on collective farm fields. The only result was that private plots produced less food, and the entire nation was the loser.

Other Khrushchev farm policies did not help matters much either. Continued attempts to dictate to the farmers what they should grow or how much land should remain fallow (not planted with crops but allowed to remain as grassland) did far more harm than good. So did another of Khrushchev's administrative reforms. In 1961 he decided that the reason the Ministry of Agriculture was doing so poorly was that it was located in a city—Moscow—rather than in the countryside, where it belonged. He therefore insisted that the entire ministry be located on a huge state farm about 60 miles (96 km) from the capital.

Since everything, as usual, had to be done immediately, ministry workers soon found themselves commuting for more than four hours a day, back and forth to offices lacking basic facilities, even telephones. On top of that, the officials were expected to do farm chores. This supposedly would keep them in better touch with the problems farmers faced.

Not satisfied with uprooting the ministry responsible for agriculture in the country as a whole, Khrushchev insisted that the republic-level ministries relocate to the countryside as well. He did the same for agricultural schools, succeeding mainly in disrupting their operations.

Uncooperative weather added to Khrushchev's agricultural problems. Since the 1950s he had been forcing the country's farmers to plant more and more corn, which requires hot and humid weather to thrive. In 1962 cool, rainy summer weather killed up to 80 percent of the corn in the European part of the country. In the Virgin Lands things were even worse. The region consistently failed to meet its production quotas. There the weather was too *dry*. The summer of 1962 saw windstorms that caused extensive erosion. In 1963 disaster struck. Dry conditions and winds of up to 95 miles (152 km) per hour produced a dust bowl. Topsoil was blown away and millions of acres of farmland ruined. Entire towns were covered with silt. It was a major ecological disaster.

All of this had its effects well beyond the farms. In 1962 the rising cost of agricultural goods forced the state to raise food prices. This led to many protests and strikes. The worst occurred in the city of Novocherkassk. There a protest parade carrying pictures of Lenin was fired on by troops, killing at least seventy demonstrators. Then the drought of 1963 threatened widespread shortages and hunger. To avoid this, the Soviet government had to undergo the humiliation of buying food from the United States and other capitalist countries, nations the Soviets liked to insist were on an unstoppable decline.

When dealing with people rather than crops, Khrushchev

implemented policies in these years that often were harsh or erratic. In terms of religion and religious minorities, the watchword was repression. Beginning with a new law in 1961, the pressures against the practice of religion increased. New restrictions were placed on the teaching of religion. More than ten thousand Orthodox churches were closed over the next several years, and many were demolished.

Although all religions felt the pressure, the Jewish faith was singled out for the most severe persecution. Between 1961 and 1963 there was a campaign against what the Soviets called "economic crimes." Over one hundred people were executed for these crimes, which involved a variety of violations. In a country where they amounted to about 1½ percent of the population, Jews accounted for over 60 percent of those executed for such crimes. In one trial in 1963, when twelve people were convicted of the same crime, only the six Jewish defendants were executed.

Khrushchev was also unpredictable in his dealings with artists and intellectuals. At times he seemed to stand firmly behind greater freedom in the arts. In 1962 he intervened personally to allow the publication of Alexander Solzhenitsyn's *One Day in the Life of Ivan Denisovich*. This small novel was a large literary and political bombshell. By exposing the horrors of Stalin's labor camps as never before, it promised expanded freedom of discussion for all Soviet citizens. At other times Khrushchev's actions were more difficult to gauge. In December of that year he visited an exhibition of modern art. He paused to criticize the work of the best-known artist there, Ernst Neizvestny. He informed the artist that his abstract work was so terrible that "a donkey could do better with its tail." But Khrushchev also took the time to talk seriously with Neizvestny. He ended the conversation in a way that could intrigue the bold while frightening the timid:

> He [Khrushchev] said, "You're an interesting man—I enjoy people like you—but inside you there are an angel

*and a devil. If the devil wins, we'll crush you. If the angel wins we'll do all we can to help you."* And he gave me his hand. [2]

Another public debate, this time with Yevgeny Yevtushenko, also sent a mixed message to the Soviet public. Yevtushenko defended modern and abstract artists, noting that any problems they had could be "straightened out in time." Khrushchev's crude reply was that "the grave straightens out the hump-backed." At that point the poet instructed the party leader that "really, there are other ways."[3] Yet after he allowed himself to be contradicted in public, Khrushchev lashed out in early 1963 at artists and intellectuals and even praised Stalin. This was followed by the arrest and trial of a brilliant young poet named Joseph Brodsky, who years later would win the Nobel Prize for literature. But even the Brodsky case showed how much things had changed. His case led to public protests from leading Soviet cultural figures, something that would have been suicidal under Stalin.

While Khrushchev struggled to reestablish his footing at home, problems abroad further complicated his life. He did not visit China after 1959, but the bad memories of that trip did not lessen with time. Mao, Khrushchev felt, was "bursting with an impatient desire to rule the world." He was a man whose "chauvinism and arrogance sent a shiver up my spine."[4] But whatever the personal dislike between the two Communist leaders, the fact is that the growing rift between their two nations ran far deeper than any antagonism between two men. The old Chinese territorial grievances remained. The Chinese were furious at Soviet attempts to improve relations with the United States. They felt contempt for the Soviet leadership's concern with raising material living standards at the expense, the Chinese felt, of revolutionary idealism. As the 1960s progressed, the Chinese increasingly felt that their country, not the Soviet Union, was the proper leader of the world Communist movement.

All of this was reflected in several events during Khrushchev's last three years in office. In 1962 the Soviets refused to support China in its border war with India. The Chinese responded in 1963 by publicly calling for changes in the Sino-Soviet border for the first time. Much more worrisome for the Soviets was the Chinese explosion of their first atomic bomb in 1964.

Troubles with Communist China were matched by troubles with the United States. Although both men had sincerely hoped to improve Soviet-American relations, Khrushchev's relationship with President Eisenhower had ended on a sour note when the latter left office in January 1961. That same note sounded again with the new American administration of President John F. Kennedy. Khrushchev has always claimed that he liked and respected Kennedy. The two men met briefly during Khrushchev's 1959 American tour, and Khrushchev remembered that the young and handsome American senator had made a favorable impression on him. During Kennedy's 1960 election campaign against the man Khrushchev called "that son of a bitch Richard Nixon,"5 the Soviets did not release downed U-2 pilot Gary Powers. Khrushchev maintained that this was because he did not want to help Nixon by giving the Republican party a foreign policy success during the election. (Powers was released shortly after the election.) Khrushchev also noted in his memoirs that he was greatly saddened by Kennedy's assassination in November 1963, and there is no reason not to take him at his word.

Nevertheless, as national leaders, Khrushchev and Kennedy got off on the wrong foot. In June 1961 the two men went to Vienna to "get acquainted." The meeting did not go well.

*President Kennedy and Khrushchev share a laugh during the first few minutes of the Vienna talks.*

Khrushchev immediately put pressure on Kennedy to get Western troops out of West Berlin. He badgered the American president on several other points as well and seems to have come away from the meeting thinking he could push Kennedy around. A Soviet diplomat who later defected to the West quoted Khrushchev as calling Kennedy "wishy-washy" and observing: "I know for certain that Kennedy doesn't have a backbone, nor, generally speaking, does he have the courage to stand up to a serious challenge."[6] Kennedy seemed to confirm that he had failed to impress the Soviet leader. He complained to an advisor: "If Khrushchev wants to rub my nose in the dirt, it's all over. That son of a bitch won't pay any attention to words. He has to see you move."[7]

It turned out that Khrushchev was the first to move. By the summer of 1961 he had a genuine crisis on his hands, involving Berlin. The city Khrushchev called America's "blister" in Europe was also the Soviet Union's ulcer, and by July 1961 it was bleeding uncontrollably. Ten thousand East Germans per *week*, many of them young skilled workers, were fleeing their country to the West by crossing from East Berlin into West Berlin. This was possible because there were no barriers between the two Berlins, and leaving for the West was as easy as taking a subway ride.

Suddenly, on August 13, 1961, Khrushchev acted to close the wound. The Soviets and East Germans began building the Berlin Wall, a barrier that soon cut through the heart of the former capital of Germany and cut off the escape route to the West.

Kennedy could not respond. The wall was on East German territory. Once again Khrushchev got the better of the young American president but only in terms of actually being able to build the wall. The Berlin Wall immediately became and has remained a symbol of Communist failure, of a system that had to build a wall to keep its people from running away. It was a point Kennedy made with great effect in June 1963, when he went to the Wall and declared to a huge rally: *"Ich bin ein Berliner"* (I am a Berliner).

Khrushchev also got to see Berlin and its wall but only under cover. In what must qualify as the most remarkable of Khrushchev's many on-the-spot tours, he secretly visited West Berlin. Taking advantage of the Soviet military's right to enter West Berlin, Khrushchev accompanied a Soviet officer into the city. Khrushchev never got out of the car. Still, he recalled with the pride of someone who feels he got away with something, "I made a full tour and saw what the city was like."[8]

Then Khrushchev reached too far, to within 90 miles (144 km) of America's Florida coast. He was reaching for the island nation of Cuba, where Fidel Castro had set up a Communist government. American hostility to the Castro regime had led to Kennedy's supporting an invasion of the island by Cuban exiles in 1961. The invaders were crushed at their starting point, the Bay of Pigs, leaving Kennedy embarrassed, angry, and determined to redeem himself. Cuba, then, was a dangerous place for Nikita Khrushchev to cause Kennedy any more trouble.

But Khrushchev was not deterred. During the spring of 1962, having consulted only with a small group of advisors and colleagues, he decided to place intermediate-range ballistic missiles (those with a range up to 1,500 miles [2,400 km]) in Cuba. These missiles were capable of carrying nuclear warheads. Khrushchev made this decision because he faced several problems. First, Khrushchev and his advisors feared and expected another invasion of Castro's island, this one a direct attack by American troops. The Soviets very much wanted to protect the Castro regime, which was the first Communist foothold in the Western Hemisphere and therefore one of the Soviet Union's major foreign policy successes since World War II. The planned missiles could be expected to prevent such an attack. Second, these missiles would have another important payoff. The Soviet Union lagged far behind the United States in developing intercontinental ballistic missiles, those with a range of over 5,000 miles (8,000 km). This left the Americans able to attack the Soviet Union with nuclear missiles based safely on American territory, while the Soviets lacked a similar capacity.

Khrushchev was under pressure to do something about this. Moving intermediate-range missiles to Cuba would accomplish several things. It would give the Soviet Union the capacity to hit the United States with these shorter-range missiles until the new intercontinental missiles were ready. Aside from giving Khrushchev an instant solution to his country's weakness relative to the United States, this strategy would be a relatively cheap solution as well. This suited Khrushchev's constant desire to avoid spending too much on the military lest he starve his domestic programs. At the same time, Khrushchev would also be able to silence his critics within the Communist camp, both at home and in China, who were accusing him of being too soft on the capitalist enemy.

Missiles in Cuba, Khrushchev calculated, also would give the Americans, "some of their own medicine." Khrushchev had in mind several American military bases and nuclear weapons in countries bordering on the Soviet Union, especially the American intermediate-range nuclear missiles in Turkey.

The Cuban Missile Crisis that resulted from this most daring of Khrushchev's many gambles lasted thirteen days, October 16 through 28, 1962. It brought the two superpowers to the very brink of war, as close as they have ever come. On October 16, President Kennedy was shown convincing evidence that Soviet missile bases were being built in Cuba. He responded several days later by announcing a naval blockade of the island. It was now up to Khrushchev whether to challenge the blockade and risk nuclear war or to order Soviet ships en route to Cuba to turn back before they reached the U.S. warships surrounding the island.

The pressure built to incredible proportions as messages flew back and forth across the Atlantic. Apparently the Soviets were shocked by Kennedy's strong response. They had made no plans for what to do if they ran into trouble. Khrushchev tried to mask his concern by publicly going about business as usual. The result was that the Soviet leadership experienced a kind of cultural vacation. Trying to look calm and confident, Khrushchev and four top leaders attended the opera on October 23. Khrushchev even made a point of visiting the performers backstage. Three days later the same men were at a concert. On the 28th no less than ten leaders, including Khrushchev, showed up at the theater. But Khrushchev was hardly enjoying himself. A better indication of his mood was the fitful night he spent in his Kremlin office sleeping on a couch with his clothes on.

In fact, the world came closer to war than even the Soviet and American leaders knew, for they were not always in control of activities they thought they were managing. At one point the American navy had vessels farther out from the Cuban coast than Kennedy had wanted. This was dangerous because it brought American and Soviet ships closer together and so cut down on the time the two sides had to work out a solution. At another point the American nuclear bomber force went on a high alert. This move, which naturally frightened the Soviets, was done on orders of the top American air force general, *without* authorization from President Kennedy. Just as negotiations were reaching a critical stage, an American U-2 reconnaissance plane was shot down over Cuba. To this day it is unknown whether the Cubans or the Soviets were responsible for that provocative act.

It also appears that a key Soviet negotiator threatened a Soviet blockade of Berlin, and, without first consulting Khrushchev, he demanded that the United States withdraw its missiles from Turkey. Meanwhile, the United States had to cope with the terrifying uncertainty of not knowing whether the nuclear *warheads* for the Soviet missiles were already in Cuba. Not knowing, the American leaders were forced to assume that the warheads were in fact there. This pushed the finger that much closer to the war button. In Washington plans went ahead to bomb the missile sites and invade Cuba if the Soviets did not agree to remove the missiles. Almost twenty-five years later the Soviets revealed that twenty nuclear warheads had arrived in Cuba before Kennedy proclaimed his blockade, although they had never been attached to the missiles assigned to carry them to their targets.

While the Americans in Washington were guessing and preparing for the worst, Khrushchev was having troubles of another kind in Moscow. He was under attack from his own military and other hard-line forces who did not want to compromise. At least one peculiar event showed how much trouble he was in. On October 25 the Ukrainian town of Khrushchev suddenly changed its name to Kremges. Meanwhile the military newspaper *Red Star* was taking a much harder line on the crisis than the official government paper, *Izvestiya*. It is therefore reasonable to believe Khrushchev's claim that he had to go against his own military in working out a compromise with Kennedy. As Khrushchev later recalled:

> So I said to myself, "To hell with those maniacs. If I can get the United States to assure me that it will not attempt to overthrow the Cuban government, I will remove the missiles."[9]

It was not quite that easy, however. It is clear that Khrushchev had to reach deep down to find the strength and wisdom to overcome this crisis. A long, rambling letter he wrote to Kennedy on October 26 indicates how strained Khrushchev was.

> You can be confident that we are quite sane and understand clearly that if we attack you, you will retaliate. But we will match you blow for blow. And I believe that you are fully aware of this, which indicates that we are normal people, that we understand the position and can assess the

*situation accurately. Why, then, should we court disaster, as you seem to imagine we are doing. Only a lunatic or suicide would do that, someone bent on his own destruction and that of the world before he dies.*[10]

Khrushchev then offered a suggestion that proved to be the basis of the eventual settlement. The Soviet Union agreed to remove its missiles from Cuba. In return the United States pledged not to invade the island. The Americans also agreed to remove some obsolete missiles in Turkey, ones that Kennedy had wanted removed well before the Cuban crisis. The United States insisted, however, that the removal of the Turkish missiles not be publicly linked to the Cuban situation. If the Soviets did so, Kennedy warned, the agreement over the Turkish missiles would be off.

The crisis was over. The U.S. Secretary of State Dean Rusk observed that the two nations had been "eyeball to eyeball" and it was the Soviets who blinked. In truth, this most dangerous of Soviet/American confrontations ended as a draw. Khrushchev won a promise from the Americans not to invade Cuba and therefore could claim that he had achieved a victory. But it was the Soviets that backed down—in front of the world—on their second objective: to be able to threaten the United States from 90 miles (144 km) away. Khrushchev had to retreat because of overwhelming American nuclear strength and Kennedy's obvious determination not to give in.

Still, Khrushchev had pushed to the very limit. Walt Rostow, one of Kennedy's top advisors during the crisis, summed up Khrushchev and his behavior well when he wrote: "Khrushchev, that complex, humane gambler bandit, did not stop until he felt the knife on his skin."[11]

There were some positive results from the Cuban Missile Crisis. Both sides worked to draw back from the brink. A direct telephone hot line was established between the Kremlin and the White House. In August 1963 the Soviet Union and the

United States, joined by Great Britain, signed a partial nuclear test ban treaty. This treaty banned the testing of nuclear weapons in the atmosphere, under water, and in space.

This was good news for both the Soviet Union and the United States. Khrushchev's problem was that he did not have much to go along with it in the years after his Cuban misadventure. He could point with pride to the growth of heavy industry—coal, steel, electricity, cement, etc.—by 50 percent between 1958 and 1963. But growth rates for *all* industrial production for 1963 and 1964 were the worst since Stalin's death. Meanwhile agricultural production for 1963 was below 1962 levels. The serious food shortages that resulted led directly to the huge purchases of foreign grain in the fall of 1963.

It seems that by 1963 and certainly by 1964 almost every powerful interest group in the Soviet Union had a reason to be angry with Nikita Khrushchev. The military was upset that Khrushchev had stunted its growth. It felt he had caused the Cuban humiliation: the Soviet Union having to back down in the face of superior American strength. Government officials were upset with Khrushchev's erratic economic policies. Many of them had opposed the creation of Khrushchev's 105 *sovnarkhozy*—the local economic councils—in 1957. The councils had not worked well, so in 1963 Khrushchev combined many of them, reducing their number to forty-seven. Done hastily, this caused much confusion because the new *sovnarkhozy* borders did not conform to any other administrative boundaries. This further angered and frustrated the government officials who somehow had to make the unwieldy system work.

Nor was Khrushchev doing well among party officials. He angered them back in 1961 with a new rule adopted at the Twenty-second Party Congress. Rule 25 called for limits on the terms of party officials. It would help Khrushchev move his supporters into key positions and prevent them from becoming too powerful at his expense. But it also cut at the job security party officials expected and demanded and therefore was extremely unpopular.

Even more unpopular was the most radical of Khrushchev's many administrative reforms. Late in 1962 he split the Communist party in half! One branch of the newly split party was to be responsible for agriculture, the other for industry. Khrushchev's intent was that this more direct responsibility and focus would promote efficiency. It had the opposite effect. Each half of the party tended to ignore the needs of the other. Since each region and district suddenly had *two* first secretaries, it was impossible to know who was in charge. The result was that often nobody was, especially when it came to services that were neither industrial nor agricultural, such as education or health care. More than anything else, Khrushchev's splitting of the party made him enemies and cut him off from what had once been his main base of support. Nor was Khrushchev, the man who had promised prosperity so often, popular with ordinary citizens as they chased after scarce food, put up with defective consumer goods, or watched their real incomes fall in the face of rising prices.

During 1964 Khrushchev was busy as usual, touring, visiting abroad, and planning new policies. Others were busy as well. They were the top officials in the Presidium, and their plans concerned the removal from office of First Secretary Nikita Khrushchev.

There were warning signs for those with eyes to see. At the end of September 1964 a late-night call came to Khrushchev's villa overlooking the Moscow River. Since Khrushchev himself was not at home, his son Sergei took the call. The unfamiliar voice on the other end belonged to a man named Vasily Golyukov. He was the bodyguard of one of the plotters, an official named Nikolai Ignatev, whom Khrushchev had demoted from the Presidium three years earlier. Golyukov told

Sergei the names of several key plotters: Ignatev; Presidium members Leonid Brezhnev and Nikolai Podgorny; Central Committee secretary Alexandr Shelepin; and KGB chief Vladimir Y. Semichastny.

Sergei had two problems. He was absolutely barred from discussing Presidium members with anyone, and he was in the position of having to accuse some of his father's closest associates of plotting against him. It took several days for Sergei to work up the courage to bring up the matter with his father. The senior Khrushchev's reaction was disbelief. He did agree to have Sergei and Golyukov pass the information to Anastas Mikoyan, another Presidium member, and to have Mikoyan investigate the matter. Khrushchev then promptly left for a well-deserved vacation at a Black Sea resort.

Other signs of trouble popped up, which Khrushchev also ignored. A security ship unexpectedly appeared offshore near Khrushchev's resort, and remained. First Secretary of the Communist Party and Prime Minister of the Soviet Union Nikita Khrushchev somehow was not informed when the Soviet space program scored a major triumph by launching three cosmonauts. Khrushchev had to phone the space officials himself to find out what was going on.

Then came a call from Mikhail Suslov, a powerful Presidium member and chief Kremlin ideologist. He told Khrushchev to come to Moscow immediately for an urgent meeting on agriculture that the Presidium was holding. When Khrushchev objected, he was told the meeting would go on without him if he did not return. By then the unpleasant signs could not be ignored. Turning to Mikoyan, who had joined him on vacation, Khrushchev remarked: "They don't have any urgent agricultural problems. I think this call was connected with what Sergei warned us about."[12]

When Khrushchev arrived in Moscow on October 13, he found that nobody on the Presidium, with the temporary exception of Mikoyan, supported him. After holding out for one day, Khrushchev "voluntarily" gave up his posts and resigned on October 14 at a Central Committee meeting from which all of his supporters were excluded. Leonid Brezhnev, a long-time supporter whom Khrushchev had promoted many times, succeeded him as First Secretary. Alexander Kosygin, another man who had risen to the party's top ranks under Khrushchev, replaced him as prime minister.

Khrushchev was bowing to the reality of overwhelming opposition to him when he gave up power on October 14. Still, it was out of character for Nikita Khrushchev, always the fighter and survivor, to give up without a struggle. Two factors might account for this. First, there was the important matter of party loyalty, something drilled into every party member since Lenin's day. As Sergei Khrushchev recorded in his diary:

> My father said at the Presidium meeting that he was not about to engage in a power struggle since he considered it impossible to go against the opinion of a majority. He had talked of the role of the party and the necessity to preserve the unity of its ranks, which would have been impossible had there been a power struggle at the highest echelons of the leadership. [13]

Perhaps more important, Khrushchev seemed to have lost the will for the bitter political struggle it would have taken to try to survive. Although he was in relatively good health and still could work long, hard days, Khrushchev was seventy years old. His eyesight was weakening. As Sergei put it, Nikita Khrushchev, however reluctantly and even bitterly, seemed to have "understood it was time to go."[14]

Khrushchev's final defeat has been called his "finest hour." He himself probably best explained why. When he arrived home the day of his removal from office he remarked:

*Well, that's it. I'm retired now. Perhaps the most important thing I did was just this—that they were able to get rid of me simply by voting, whereas Stalin would have had them all arrested.*[15]

In other words, a fundamental change had taken place in the Soviet Union while Nikita Khrushchev governed. The country now had rules by which people could guide their lives and find security. The explosive and unpredictable violence that raged through Soviet society under Stalin had been eliminated. It is fitting that in 1964 the main beneficiary of this change, beginning an unwanted but still quite comfortable retirement, was Nikita Sergeyevich Khrushchev himself.

# EPILOGUE

Nikita Khrushchev was removed from office on October 14, 1964. The next day the official announcement claimed that the ex-First Secretary, who could still work a fifteen-hour day, had resigned because of "deteriorating health." On October 17 *Pravda* gave a more truthful account of what had happened. It denounced the fallen Khrushchev for

> *hare-brained schemes; half-baked conclusions and hasty decisions and actions, divorced from reality; bragging and bluster; attraction to rule by fiat; unwillingness to take into account what science and practical experience have already discovered.* [1]

This was followed by a quick reversal of some of his more controversial policies, among them his thoroughly unpopular decision to split the party into agricultural and industrial halves.

After the attacks on him in the press at the time of his fall, Khrushchev ceased to be mentioned by the Soviet media at all. In effect, he became a "nonperson." Although this was a rather severe punishment for a man who so enjoyed being in the limelight, Khrushchev did not suffer in a material sense. He was given a country home with a plot of land, as well as an apartment in Moscow and the use of a car and driver. He also received a twenty-four-hour guard, something he may not have appreciated but that did not interfere with his movements.

It took Khrushchev a while to recover from the shock of his removal from office. But he was too vigorous a man to mope for long. Khrushchev began to read a great deal. He listened to foreign radio broadcasts, the very same ones he had jammed when he had been in charge, to find out as much as he could about world affairs. He developed a new hobby—photography—and apparently became quite good at it.

Khrushchev also remained an avid gardener and farmer. He continued to experiment with various strains of corn, as well as with other crops and new agricultural methods he heard about. Many hours were enjoyably spent talking with local farmers in the area of his cottage, offering advice, criticizing if he found something wrong, and simply passing the time. Sometimes he and Nina Petrovna went to Moscow for cultural events, although Khrushchev preferred not to spend much time in his apartment there.

Khrushchev returned to the public eye only once before his death, when his memoirs were published in the West. He seems to have decided to write them after he read memoirs written by other political figures of his era and was not pleased by what they said. When he was denied a secretary to take down his words, Khrushchev responded by using a tape recorder to dictate his reminiscences. Their publication in the West in 1970 caused a storm at home. The Soviet government claimed they were a forgery. After a heated session with an important Politburo member, Khrushchev signed a statement condemning what he called their unauthorized publication.

Toward the end of his life Khrushchev thought about the arms race and the threat it represented to humanity. He called it

*Nikita Khrushchev (wearing medals) and his family in 1964. His daughters Yelena and Rada (second and third from left, consecutively) and son Sergei (third from right) are the children from Khrushchev's second marriage to Nina P. Kukharchuk (fourth from left).*

a "vicious circle" and "idiotic."[2] He urged his country to take a more flexible attitude toward arms control. But Khrushchev's successors paid no attention to his concerns as the arms race spiraled upward at an ever faster pace.

On his seventy-fifth birthday in 1969, Khrushchev received greetings from important people all over the world. He even received a phone call from members of the staff of *Izvestiya*, the official government newspaper. But by 1970 his health was clearly failing, and he had a heart attack. He weakened further during the summer of 1971. On September 11, 1971, at the age of seventy-seven, Nikita Khrushchev died.

In death, as in the last years of his life, Khrushchev remained out of favor. *Pravda* noted his death with only a six-line announcement that the party's former First Secretary and "personal pensioner," Nikita Khrushchev, had died. Khrushchev was not interned in the Kremlin wall, the traditional resting place for leading Soviet heroes. Instead he was buried in the cemetery of the Novodevichy Monastery, a place reserved for important people of lesser rank. The new party leadership sent a large wreath, but none of them attended the funeral. Some of the people Khrushchev had released from the Gulag did show up. But they, along with all Soviet citizens except his family and a few close friends, were not allowed into the cemetery for the burial. The official reason was that it just happened to be closed for a "cleaning day."

Foreign journalists were allowed at the gravesite. They heard Sergei Khrushchev deliver a short eulogy for his father:

> *We simply want to say a few words about the man whom we are burying now, and for whom we are crying. . . . I won't talk about the great statesman. . . . In recent days the newspapers of the whole world, with rare exceptions, talked about this. I will not evaluate the contributions which Nikita Sergeyevich, my father, made. I don't have the right to do that. History will do that. . . .*

*The only thing I can say is that he left no one indifferent. There are people who loved him and people who hated him, but no one can pass him by without turning to look. . . . A man has gone from us who had the right to be called a man. Unfortunately, there are very few such real people.*[3]

After his moving statement, Sergei Khrushchev still had one more thing to do for his father. He went to see Ernst Neizvestny, the sculptor and artist whose work Khrushchev had so insultingly denounced almost ten years earlier. It appeared that the retired old man had experienced a change of heart. In his father's will, Sergei told Neizvestny, it was written that Neizvestny should create Khrushchev's tombstone. Neizvestny agreed. A scene then took place that Khrushchev certainly would have approved of:

*Sergei Khrushchev and I [Neizvestny] went back to Sergei's flat with five of our friends. He took out a bottle of brandy that President De Gaulle had given to Khrushchev—the brandy was a hundred years old—and said to us, "My father could never bring himself to drink this expensive brandy. Today we'll drink it." And we polished the bottle off.*[4]

It took three years for the family to get permission to place Neizvestny's work over Khrushchev's grave. It is a handsome bronze bust surrounded by two interlocking marble columns: one white, the other black. The columns clearly and dramatically represent the positive and negative sides of Khrushchev's career.

In terms of both how the sculptor was chosen and what he created, it was a most fitting monument to Khrushchev. His legacy is undeniably a mixed one. Yet the passage of time—and the judgment of "history" his son mentioned—has been kind

*Ernst Neizvestny was commissioned to build Khrushchev's
tombstone, shown here as a geometrical piece of sculpture
showcasing a bronze bust of the controversial Soviet leader.*

to Khrushchev. When placed against the background of his times and what has happened in the Soviet Union since his fall, it is his virtues and accomplishments rather than his faults and failures that stand out.

The overriding problem of the Khrushchev era was how to reform the Stalinist system without undermining it. There was general agreement that government by terror had to end, and the nation's low standard of living had to be raised. Beyond that there was little agreement.

Khrushchev's great strength was that more than any other Soviet leader he was willing to face the problems directly. That is why he denounced Stalin in 1956 despite strong opposition in the Presidium. That is also why he appealed directly to the Soviet population at large. Khrushchev was no democrat. He was no more ready than his colleagues to let the people decide. Still, at least he knew firsthand how they lived. No matter how powerful he became, he never stopped trudging through muddy wheat fields or poking his head into the corners of grimy factories. He never became too important to talk to ordinary Soviet citizens, to encourage them, criticize them, and, on occasion, even listen to them.

In the end Khrushchev stumbled and was removed from office. Many of his policies were then reversed by his successors. But both the Soviet elite that removed him and the population at large that greeted his downfall so indifferently owed Nikita Khrushchev a considerable debt. Although he did not change the fundamental structure of Soviet society, he played a pivotal role in ending the most unbearable hardships of the Stalin era. The secret police terror was curbed and the major part of the Gulag slave labor network dismantled. A serious and reasonably successful effort was made to raise the standard of living. The country enjoyed a genuine cultural reawakening. Under Khrushchev life in the Soviet Union became better for almost everyone, no small achievement for any national leader.

It would take the passage of a generation for Khrushchev to be rescued from historical banishment. The process began in

1985 with the selection of Mikhail Gorbachev as general secretary of the Communist party. Gorbachev's generation began their political careers in the mid-1950s. He and his colleagues are appropriately known as the "children of the Twentieth Party Congress." Gorbachev himself pointed this out in a speech he made in 1987 near Moscow. He mentioned Khrushchev by name and commented that party activists of his own generation had begun their careers at the time of the Twentieth Party Congress. Gorbachev was too low on the party ladder to be at that congress, but he was a delegate in the hall at the Twenty-second Congress, when Khrushchev delivered his second great attack on Stalin.

There can be little doubt that Gorbachev has been influenced by Khrushchev. Gorbachev is smoother, more sophisticated, and far better educated. Yet his hands-on, on-the-spot style of leadership, his spontaneous meetings and frank conversations with ordinary people, are vintage Khrushchev. Gorbachev has gone well beyond Khrushchev in the types of reforms he is proposing. But in daring to challenge powerful conservative party interests, Mikhail Gorbachev is following in Khrushchev's footsteps.

This would have suited Nikita Khrushchev, for he remained a believer in the ideals of his youth until the end. On the very last page of his memoirs, he observed:

> Everything I've said in my memoirs, I say as a Communist who wants a more enlightened Communist society—not for myself, because my time has already come and gone, but for my friends and for my people in the future.[5]

Khrushchev would take some satisfaction in knowing that with the rise to power of the Gorbachev generation—and the exciting new efforts toward reform at home and the dramatic improvement in Soviet-American relations that have come about as a result—his time has come again.

# SOURCE NOTES

## CHAPTER ONE

1. Anton Chekhov, "Peasants," in *Anton Chekhov: Selected Stories*, translated by Ann Dunnigan (New York: New American Library, 1960), p. 273.
2. Quoted in Harold H. Martin, "Back to the Beginning of the Tumultuous Life of Nikita Khrushchev," *The Saturday Evening Post*, November 7, 1964, p. 19.
3. Ibid.
4. Quoted in Lazar Pistrak, *The Grand Tactician: Khrushchev's Rise to Power* (New York: Frederick A. Praeger, 1961), p. 4.
5. Martin, "Back to the Beginning," p. 23.
6. Nikita Khrushchev, *Khrushchev Remembers*, Introduction, Commentary, and Notes by Edward Crankshaw, translated and edited by Strobe Talbott (New York: Bantam Books, 1971), p. 20 (hereafter cited as *Khrushchev Remembers*).
7. Ibid.
8. Ibid., p. 21.

## CHAPTER TWO

1. William Henry Chamberlin, *The Russian Revolution*, vol. 2 (New York: Grosset and Dunlop, 1965), pp. 335, 356.
2. *Khrushchev Remembers*, p. 12.
3. Ibid.

4. Ibid., p. 18.
5. Quoted in Pistrak, *Grand Tactician*, p. 19.
6. Quoted in Martin, "Back to the Beginning," p. 24.
7. Quoted in Pistrak, *Grand Tactician*, p. 21.
8. *Khrushchev Remembers*, pp. 22–23.
9. Quoted in Pistrak, *Grand Tactician*, p. 31.
10. *Khrushchev Remembers*, p. 28.
11. Ibid., pp. 224, 232.
12. Ibid., p. 32.

## CHAPTER THREE

1. Victor Kravchenko, *I Chose Justice* (New York: Charles Scribner's Sons, 1950), pp. 99–100.
2. Quoted in Moshe Lewin, *Russian Peasants and Soviet Powers: A Study of Collectivization*, translated by Irene Nove (New York: Norton, 1975), p. 506.
3. *Khrushchev Remembers*, p. 76.
4. Ibid., p. 37.
5. Ibid., p. 54.
6. Quoted in Roy Medvedev, *Khrushchev: A Biography*, translated by Brian Pearce (Garden City, N.Y.: Anchor Books, 1984), p. 16.
7. Nikita Khrushchev, *Khrushchev Remembers: The Last Testament*, translated by Strobe Talbot, Foreword by Edward Crankshaw, Introduction by Jerrold L. Schecter (Boston and Toronto: Little, Brown and Company, 1974), p. 90 (hereafter cited as *Last Testament*).
8. *Khrushchev Remembers*, p. 71.
9. Quoted in Pistrak, *Grand Tactician*, pp. 161–62.
10. Quoted in Pistrak, *Grand Tactician*, pp. 117–22.
11. Quoted in Edward Crankshaw, *Khrushchev: A Career* (New York: Viking Press, 1966), p. 120.

## CHAPTER FOUR

1. *Khrushchev Remembers*, p. 179.
2. *Pravda*, August 7, 1961.
3. Quoted in Pistrak, *Grand Tactician*, p. 218.
4. *Khrushchev Remembers*, p. 243.
5. *Last Testament*, p. 95.
6. *Khrushchev Remembers*, pp. 301–20, *passim*.
7. Svetlana Allilueva, *Twenty Letters to a Friend*, translated by Priscilla Johnson (New York: Harper & Row, 1967), p. 10.

## CHAPTER FIVE

1. *Khrushchev Remembers*, p. 366.
2. Quoted in Medvedev, *Khrushchev*, p. 67.
3. *Last Testament*, p. 123.
4. *Khrushchev Remembers*, pp. 432–34.
5. Ibid., p. 438.
6. Quoted in Medvedev, *Khrushchev*, p. 89.
7. *Khrushchev Remembers*, p. 382.
8. "Khrushchev's Secret Speech" (as released by the U.S. Department of State, June 4, 1956), in *Khrushchev Remembers*, p. 620.
9. Quoted in Medvedev, *Khrushchev*, p. 100.
10. *Khrushchev Remembers*, p. 462.
11. Quoted in Edward Crankshaw, *Khrushchev*, p. 250.

## CHAPTER SIX

1. Frank Roberts, "Encounters with Khrushchev," in *Khrushchev and Khrushchevism*, edited by Martin McCauley (Bloomington and Indianapolis, Ind.: Indiana University Press, 1987), pp. 221–22.
2. *Khrushchev Remembers*, pp. 434–35.
3. *Last Testament*, pp. 424, 430.
4. Ibid., p. 376.
5. Ibid., p. 457.
6. Quoted in Sidney Ploss, *Conflict and Decision-Making in Soviet Russia: A Case Study of Agricultural Policy, 1953–1963* (Princeton, N.J.: Princeton University Press, 1965), p. 149.
7. *Last Testament*, p. 132.
8. Ibid., p. 87.
9. Quoted in James B. Bruce, *The Politics of Soviet Policy Formation: Khrushchev's Innovative Policies in Education and Agriculture* (Denver: University of Denver, 1976), pp. 54, 61.
10. *Last Testament*, p. 369.
11. *Khrushchev Speaks: Selected Speeches, Articles, and Press Conferences, 1949–1961*, edited by Thomas P. Whitney (Ann Arbor, Mich.: University of Michigan Press, 1963), p. 355.
12. Ibid., pp. 323–24.
13. *Last Testament*, p. 402.
14. Yevgeny Yevtushenko, "Stalin's Heirs," *The Poetry of Yevgeny Yevtushenko* (New York: October House, 1965), pp. 41–42.

## CHAPTER SEVEN

1. *New York Times*, July 31, 1961, quoted in James E. McSherry, *Khrushchev and Kennedy in Retrospect* (New York: Open-Door Press, 1971), p. 62.
2. *Vremya i My* (Tel Aviv), no. 41, 1979, p. 176, quoted in Medvedev, *Khrushchev*, p. 218.
3. Quoted in Priscilla Johnson, *Khrushchev and the Arts: The Politics of Soviet Culture* (Cambridge, Mass.: MIT Press, 1965), p. 121.
4. *Khrushchev Remembers*, p. 524.
5. Ibid., p. 507.
6. Arkady N. Shevchenko, *Breaking with Moscow* (New York: Alfred A. Knopf, 1985), p. 117.
7. Arthur M. Schlesinger, *A Thousand Days* (Boston: Houghton, Mifflin, 1965), p. 259.
8. *Khrushchev Remembers*, p. 506.
9. Quoted in Richard Garthoff, *Reflections on the Cuban Missile Crisis* (Washington, D.C.: Brookings Institute, 1987), p. 48.
10. Quoted in Medvedev, *Khrushchev*, p. 190.
11. Walt W. Rostow, *The Diffusion of Power* (New York: Macmillan, 1972), pp. 210–11.
12. Quoted in *Newsweek*, October 24, 1988.
13. Quoted in *New York Times*, October 23, 1988.
14. Ibid.
15. Quoted in Medvedev, *Khrushchev*, p. 245.

## EPILOGUE

1. *Pravda*, October 17, 1964.
2. *Last Testament*, p. 533.
3. Robert G. Kaiser, *Russia: The People and the Power* (New York: Atheneum, 1976), pp. 211–12.
4. Ernst Neizvestny, *Vremya i My*, quoted in Medvedev, *Khrushchev*, pp. 259–60.
5. Ibid., p. 542.

# INDEX